The Story o
Aylesford Church Organ

The People & the Music from Victorian Times to the Present

Michael J Keays

(2nd edition)

The Story of Aylesford Church Organ, originally published as
A History of the Organ at the Church of St Peter & St Paul, Aylesford, Kent.
Michael J Keays

1st edition: 1988, 2002 & 2008 (reset with minor corrections)
2nd edition: 2015 (revised, enlarged and retitled)

Published by Enso Publishing
First published 2015
© Michael J Keays, 2015

Designed and typeset by John Devlin at The Design Practice – www.thedesignpractice.co.uk

ISBN: 978-0-9567194-2-3

British Library Cataloguing in Publication Data.
A catalogue record for this book is available from the British Library.

Contents

Part 3: 1965–Present

Appendices

Introduction to the 2nd edition

It has been 27 years since I first researched and documented my findings on this delightful instrument. In that time, and with 30 years of service at Aylesford Church in September, I have discovered plenty more facts about the organ, made numerous observations, and uncovered many interesting anecdotes. I have been able to resolve some things which were uncertain in 1988, and to learn a great deal more about the technical detail of this organ. It is good to be able to finally go through my large 'jiffy' bags of notes (and countless 'post-its'), saved over the years as observations or discoveries were made. It is also good to be able to clarify some of the more technical details in tables (included within the appendices), and to share some of the many photographs given to me, shared with me, or taken over the years, including some historic ones dating back over 100 years.

The timing of this edition is of course very significant, not least because it marks the completion of a major overhaul, and the start of Aylesford organ's next chapter. Most significantly though, 2015 marks the 150th anniversary of the creation of the instrument: A century and a half after that Victorian legacy, we are able to look back at the central role played by the organ in the life of Aylesford church, a role which it is now ready to continue for a further 50 or more years.

The process of raising funds for the current restoration has been arduous – although I have discovered that this is nothing new in Aylesford. The realisation of the restoration project attests greatly to the massive effort of the parish, of the sharing of the vision and of their undaunted faith that it was quite within our reach, even if this was going to be an uphill struggle; it also reaffirms the centrality of the organ to support the regular worship of the parish. The present vicar, Rev Chris van Straaten, has been staunchly behind the project from the start, providing welcome encouragement and fundraising ideas at the times when fundraising was in danger of stalling.

This revised edition is a complete re-write of the 1988 history: It extends the 1988 text to consider tangential subjects, such as the Victorian west end gallery, and includes more extensive background material on the main organ builders associated with this organ, and on life in the parish in Victorian times; it also covers the history of the instrument as it has evolved over the last 27 years, up to the current rebuild.

The revision would not have been possible without the support of countless people, acknowledged later. I am privileged to have this support, and the opportunity to play such a fine instrument on a regular basis. As custodian of the organ in Aylesford, I trust that the recent restoration, the setting-up of a maintenance fund, the fully documented organ history and the collection of hundreds of photographs and many hours of audio recordings, will provide a lasting legacy for future generations. As the Kent Messenger wrote, in 1965, this is "one of the finest parish church organs in the county".

Michael J Keays
(Organist & Choirmaster)
March 2015

MICHAEL J KEAYS

Great divisional pipework, 2015

Introduction to the 1st edition (1988), abridged

"Opened by Mr Hopkins, Dec. 1 1865" is the final addition to entry No 375, ledger 338, on page 102 of the order book records of Forster & Andrews, organ builders of Hull.

This is the same instrument that can be heard week by week in this ancient church to this day, both for the accompaniment and embellishment of religious services, as well as for concerts.

I do not claim to be an historian – although I have a great interest in this discipline – merely an organist whose fortune it is to be in a position to use this splendid instrument. It is for this reason that I have written this historical guide. If you feel that

Cover of the 1st edition

anything has been omitted – or that you have any interesting anecdotes – do let me know. I am indebted to many people for their assistance in supplying information, and I record their names at the end of this guide.

I shall endeavour to trace the history of the organ, including answering questions that have arisen in my own mind, looking at the decoration of the instrument, its positioning and the organists.

Michael J Keays
(Organist & Choirmaster)
1988

General notes

The main detailed changes since the 1988 edition are certainty over where the organ was originally built, how it was extended and when it was moved. It is now also certain when the angels were added and when the choir was formed. This second edition also contains much more information and relevant material from 1837 to the present day, and it documents the evolving history from 1988 to 2015.

In all quoted text, square brackets are used [thus] to indicate comments or clarifications by the author.

As was common at the time for men named "John", John Walmsley was known as "Jack"; likewise William E Wilson was known as "Billy", and William Linkstead as "Bill": They are referred to as "Jack", "Billy" and "Bill" respectively throughout the text, except for where quotations use their proper names.

Some spellings are inconsistent across various sources. Harold Woolley is sometimes spelt "Wooley", Jack Walmsley is sometimes spelt "Walmisley" or "Walmesley", Charles Manglesdorff is sometimes spelt "Manglesdorf", and "Culpepper" is sometimes spelt "Colepepper": Throughout the text (unless as a quotation), what is believed to be the correct spelling ("Woolley", "Walmsley", "Manglesdorff", "Culpepper") is used.

The dedication of the church appears to have changed during the 1960s from "St Peter" to "St Peter & St Paul". There appear to be no historical records of a dual patronage, and certainly prior to the 1960s it is simply "St Peter's". In the 18th century, Edward Hasted stated that "The church ... is dedicated to St Peter", and even by the late 19th century the dedication remains unaltered: A description of the Brassey Memorial window appeared in the Sussex Agricultural Express (some of the Brassey family lived in Sussex), on 18/11/1892: "... in the side lights are figures of St. Peter, the patron saint of the church, and St. Andrew, the patron saint of the diocese."; further, the Maidstone Telegraph states that the church "is dedicated to St Peter" *(14/8/1869)*. The Parish Magazine of December 1887 refers to the church as "St Peters' Aylesford", as do the Parish Magazines of 1889, and we read that "The festival of St Peter, our Patron Saint, was observed with due solemnity ..." *(Parish Magazine, August 1898)*. The church school, too, is simply "St Peters" (and remains so to this day). Parish Magazines of the late 1940s state "Parish Church (St Peter)", and the church dedication is still "St Peter's" in the Parish Magazine of December 1966, but by February 1970 it is "St Peter

& St Paul": Unfortunately no magazines from between these dates have survived, and in official records (e.g. marriage certificates), the church is referred to simply as the "Parish Church". Canon Powell's manuscript history of Aylesford, written in the 1960s (and certainly before 1964) refers to it as "St Peter & St Paul", so it is possible that it began to take-on the dual dedication verbally in the early 1960s, prior to this being recognised in published documents late in the decade.

MICHAEL J KEAYS

Aylesford Church, October 2014

The Parish Magazine itself has also undergone name changes over the years: First published in July 1865 as "Aylesford Magazine & Parish Register", it had become "The Banner of Faith" by 1892 (no magazines have survived for 1891), and between 1894 and January 1900 was "The Church Monthly". From February 1900 it was called "The Dawn of Day", but a change to the "Parish Magazine" had occurred by 1919; magazines between 1903 and 1918 have unfortunately been lost. From 1919 until some point after January 1957, it was the "Aylesford Parish Magazine", being re-named to "The Sign" by May 1961. It became "Contact" from the January 1968 edition. The term "Parish Magazine" (usually abbreviated to "PM") is used throughout the text, to avoid confusion.

What is now the Lady Chapel was, at least during Victorian times and until early in the 20th century, simply known as the "North Aisle Chancel". There is a clear reference to the "Lady Chapel" in 1907 and 1915, although the alternate use of both names continued until at least 1965, when with the organ relocated and the space could once again become a chapel. In the text, the term "Lady Chapel" is generally reserved for references since 1965.

The church restoration works of the late 1870s are often referred to as the '1878 restoration'; it is clear that these did not complete until early 1879 (probably February), thus should really be the '1878-9 restoration'. The term '1878' restoration is generally used in this text, except where '1878-9' makes for greater clarity.

The Great soundboard table, 2014

Throughout this history, monetary values are shown as recorded, including pre-decimalised £sd values. Decimal and current money equivalent values are shown, by page number, in Appendix K. However, measurements are given in both English and metric equivalents in the text itself.

A comprehensive list of sources is cited in Appendix P. Whilst every care has been taken to provide due acknowledgement, the author apologises for any unintentional errors or omissions in this list.

All proceeds from this history will be used to support both the maintenance of the Aylesford organ and wider work of Aylesford church.

The organ: A brief overview

For the benefit of those who are less familiar with the workings of a pipe organ, the following is a brief (and necessarily high level) overview, specifically relating to the organ at Aylesford Parish Church.

The console

The organ player, or organist, plays the instrument from the console, which contains keyboards, or manuals, and foot-operated pedals (the pedalboard) to control the pipes of the various sections, or divisions. The divisions controlled by the two manuals at Aylesford are the Great and the Swell (the latter being so-called as the pipework sits inside a box with shutters which can be opened or closed by the organist, to vary the volume). The pedals control the Pedal division, providing the deepest notes on the organ.

MICHAEL J KEAYS

The Mander console, 2008

Also on the console are stop tabs (on some organs, these are stop knobs, or rocker tablets, but they all do the same thing): Each of these controls a specific set, or rank, of pipes (a 'stop'), at the pitch indicated on the stop tab. For example, the Great Open Diapason 8' tab operates the Open Diapason pipes on the Great division, which sound at the pitch that they are played: Pipes marked 4' sound an octave higher, and 16' pipes an octave lower.

Pipes from one division can often be 'coupled' to another, so that the organist only has to play one manual, but can use the pipes of more than one division: Coupler tabs are provided for this purpose, e.g. "Swell to Great".

In order to make the instrument easier to operate, a number of combination pistons are provided. These pistons, located beneath the manuals and at the back of the pedalboard, can be pre-set to activate combinations of stops by division, or across the whole organ. Modern technology has enabled these to be programmable in a number of ways: On Aylesford organ, there are ten memory levels, so each of the 24 combination pistons can be programmed in any one of ten ways.

There are other features and controls on the console, but these are omitted here for the sake of clarity.

The actions taken by the organist at the console are translated electronically into a data stream and transmitted into the organ itself via a computer cable; before the 2015 rebuild, a large number of very small wires connected console and organ. In mechanical action organs, there is a direct linkage to the organ with tracker rods, but these were removed from Aylesford in the 1965 rebuild.

The organ

The action from the console is decoded in the back of the organ, and sent to the relevant part of the organ. If the organist has played G on the Great Open Diapason 8', the signal will open the G pallet inside the Great soundboard, and also move the Open Diapason 8' slider in the Great Soundboard, so that wind can pass from the inside of the soundboard into the Great Open Diapason 8' G pipe, and make it "speak". Some pipes are mounted on "off note chests", where there is no slider: For these, either an electro-pneumatic motor or an electro-magnet operates a pallet for each pipe; once opened, the wind can enter the pipe and make it "speak".

The wind is provided under constant low pressure from the bellows (filled by an electric blower now, but hand pumped until the mid 20th century); it is moved around the organ to the various soundboards and chests through complex trunking.

The pipes

There are now 1,240 pipes making-up the organ at Aylesford Church. These pipes, made of either wood or metal, vary in size and tonal quality, providing a range of tonal "colours" at various pitches. When combined, these produce the overall sound and volume the organist desires.

Most stops have a single set, or rank, of pipes, so that if one note is played, just one pipe will sound on that rank of pipes. However, some stops have more than one rank per stop. These are the Mixture stops (sometimes given alternate names), and on Aylesford organ there are now two Mixtures, one on the Great, and one on the Swell. They are both "three rank" mixtures, meaning that for every note played by the organist, three pipes sound inside the organ; these are generally tuned to high harmonics (the lowest rank usually being two octaves higher than the note played), and are intended for use in conjunction with other stops, as they provide a great deal of the "brightness" which is essential on the organ.

MICHAEL J KEAYS

Great Division pipework

The pipes displayed in the casework are a mix of speaking pipes and "dummies": The dummy pipes are not connected to any windchest and do not "speak"; they are there simply for decorative effect, to enhance the look of the organ case. Most of the dummy pipes at Aylesford are at the back of the two sides of the organ case.

The genesis of an instrument: Music in Aylesford before 1865

Although the Parish Magazine was not published until July 1865, there are a few references to music at Aylesford Church in the Vestry Minutes prior to this, and these provide interesting and enlightening reading.

In many ways, Aylesford was a typical rural parish, with the local manors at Allington and Preston Hall (situated on the opposite bank of the river to the village), a further manor at The Friars ('Aylesford Place') and a well-supported church which had stood prominently at the top of the hill for centuries.

Aylesford, late nineteenth century

The church had a gallery at the west end, removed in the church renovations of 1878-9: In a number of churches, these galleries would have accommodated a band of musicians (mainly singers, with some instrumental support, as shown in Thomas Webster's painting "The Village Choir" (mid 19th century), and described in Thomas Hardy's "Under the Greenwood Tree"). There is no evidence of this at Aylesford however, so we can only assume that until a barrel organ was introduced into the newly erected gallery in 1838, the singing would have continued a trend prevalent since Puritan days: The Psalms, arranged metrically as hymns, would be sung unaccompanied with the congregation singing in unison, line by line, copying a lead singer, or cantor. This was also the practice in reformed churches on the continent, and for the record, the author's great grandfather (François Louis Noverraz) was cantor at Lausanne Cathedral, Switzerland, for many years until his death (aged 42) in 1914.

JAMES H SEPHTON, "AROUND AYLESFORD"

Aylesford church, the north & west, 1851 E.Pretty

The first organs at Aylesford

The barrel organ

In 1838, an old two-manual barrel organ was purchased from "Mr Joseph Walker, of 166 High Holborn, London, and consisted of three barrels with twelve tunes on each, at a cost of £158 11s 6d" *(Smetham "Rambles" p.200)*. The cost was raised by subscription over the previous year. As noted later (in the section organists and assistant organists), John Wagon was appointed organist in 1837, and thus it is highly likely he was a key player in selecting the barrel organ installed the following year, and as "keeper of accounts", in charge of co-ordinating the fundraising. The barrel organ was placed in the gallery at the west end of the church.

From 1838 the music of the worship in Aylesford changed dramatically, from unaccompanied unison singing led by one person to a selection of hymns (still predominantly metrical psalms) accompanied by the 36 tunes available on the barrel organ. The limitation of 36 tunes is not as severe as might at first appear, as tunes were generally not associated with particular words as they are today; only when the first edition of Hymns Ancient and Modern was published, in 1861, were congregations provided with a more liberated approach to hymn singing.

Although the barrel organ provided valuable service for a quarter of a century, undergoing repairs in 1852, by 1863 (just two years after Hymns Ancient & Modern was published) it was clear that the development of music at Aylesford was only going to be achieved by the provision of a (fingered) pipe organ and choir: It was a common practice for Parish churches at this time to emulate the cathedral practices in worship, although in some ways, Aylesford was fairly early in moving in this direction, almost certainly influenced by Rochester Cathedral: Rev Anthony Grant, the new vicar from 1862, had been a canon at the cathedral since 1860, and would have known the cathedral organist, John Hopkins, as noted later in the section on nineteenth century organists.

It is not known what happened to the barrel organ after its removal in 1865: It is now clear that the organ which went to the church of St Mary the Virgin, Bleasby, Notts, was in fact the vicar's house organ (see below), not the barrel organ. What is certain is that the barrel organ was removed completely once the new organ arrived.

The harmonium

In 1863, a harmonium was introduced as a temporary measure into the church by Mrs Grant, wife of Rev Andrew Grant (vicar from 1862 to 1877), and installed in the gallery. The harmonium was used in preference to the barrel organ, which was by then used merely to play people out of the services: "All the evidence that I have uncovered to date seems to indicate that it [the barrel organ] was removed immediately prior to the installation of the new organ … the barrel organ was used at the end just to play people out of church." *(Ken Wells, letters, 4/2/1988)*. It is likely that the arrival of the harmonium coincided with, and was necessitated by, the use of the new Ancient and Modern hymn book. Ken Wells also noted *(letters 27/1/1988)* that a "Maidstone Kentish Journal [*sic*] report claimed that the barrel organ was still in use, though only for playing out the congregation, up to the time that the present organ was installed."

Upon the installation of the new organ in 1865, the harmonium was sold to Alfred Joy, for £12 *(Ken Wells, letters, 20/1/1988, quoting the Maidstone and Kentish Journal 11/12/1865)*. Alfred Joy is cited as one of the Parish Guardians (and also proprietor of Mid Kent Bee farm) in the Kent Messenger 1904 Directory of Maidstone. Billy Wilson recorded in the June 1952 edition of the Parish Magazine that the harmonium "was in the possession of Mr Alfred Joy for many years. It was a pedal organ with one manual". After some time with Alfred Joy, the harmonium returned to church: Ken Wells was a chorister from c 1928 until the late 1930s, under Billy Wilson's direction throughout this time, and recalled *(letters, 17/1/1988)*: "In all this time there was a harmonium in the North Chancel, just where the present console is sited [prior to the console move in 2015]. It was a single manual and operated by pedals. In those days choir practice was always held in the choir stalls, and old Billy used to bring this old harmonium round between the choir stalls so that he could better control the choir when learning any new pieces of music or anthems etc. … I cannot say when it was removed from the church or what became of it, but suspect that it was disposed of when the 1965 alterations took place."

In fact, a new harmonium was given in 1949 by Mrs Janes of Eccles (as noted below in the section "The choir and music of the parish"), so it is likely that this replaced the old harmonium (then at least 85 years old), although how long this new harmonium lasted, and what became of it, are unrecorded.

The vicar's house organ, and the connection with Bleasby

Until research for this second edition took place, it had not been known that Rev E G Marsh had an organ installed in Aylesford Vicarage. The new evidence comes from Farewell Address to the Parishioners of Bleasby, by his son (and departing vicar of Bleasby), Rev J W Marsh, on 22/9/1874. In this, he notes that an organ had been built for his grandfather, the composer John Marsh (1752-1828), at Nethersole House, in 1783. Nethersole House was situated in Wilmingswold (now called Womenswold), east of the Barham Downs, north west of Shepherdswell *(OS grid ref. TR227506)*, approx. 10 miles south west of Canterbury. John Marsh lived at Nethersole from 1781-1787 (there are memorial tablets to the Marsh family in Womenswold church) before moving to Dodo House in Chichester, where he remained until his death in 1828.

When John Marsh moved to Chichester in 1787, the organ moved with him. His son, Rev Edward Garrard Marsh inherited the organ on John Marsh's death in 1828, and had it installed, according to Rev J W Marsh "first at Yardley vicarage, in Hertfordshire; then, in 1837, at Waltham Rectory, in Lincolnshire; and lastly, in 1840, at Aylesford Vicarage, in Kent".

Gray & Davison had looked after the organ for many years, and it is thus highly likely that John Gray, founder of the company around 1741, built the organ in 1783. The firm became Gray & Davison in 1837, and we note that in 1841, Mr Williams of Gray & Davison visited Aylesford twice, at a cost of £2 2s, invoiced to the vicar, Rev E Marsh *(Gray & Davison Ledger vol 03 page 168 (repairs & alterations), 14/8/1841)*. The purpose was to make modifications and additions to the existing instrument, including the addition of a Venetian Swell (a swell box with shutters mounted horizontally, like louvre windows), a 4' Principal to the Swell, new bellows, and to undertake re-tracking. The total cost of these modifications was £49 11d; the work was completed on 11/9/1841: This now appears to refer to the house organ, rather than the barrel organ in Aylesford church.

On the death in 1862 of Rev J W Marsh's father, Rev E G Marsh (Vicar of Aylesford),

> "the organ was brought to Bleasby Vicarage. After having been rebuilt by Messrs Gray and Davison, of London, in 1869, it was by myself and my family presented to Bleasby Church, as a thank-offering to our gracious God for His great mercy in giving our people willing hearts to make suitable provision for His worship. I trust that it may for many years lead and support the voice of praise and thanksgiving in our church. There are eight stops in the great organ including the pedal pipes, and three stops in the swell." *(J W Marsh "Bleasby Farewell Address")*.

Records of Gray & Davison *(Shop book 1862-63, vol 07 page 045 job 10162, 31/10/1862)* to Rev J W Marsh (totalling £8/1/8), show when the Aylesford Vicarage organ was removed, shortly after the death of J W Marsh's father:

To stock.

Travelling & taking down & removing organ from Aylesford	£2/16/8
Cartage	£5/5/–

A further ledger entry of Gray & Davison *(Ledger vol 07 page 228 job 10162)* to Rev J W Marsh (totalling £160/1/2), dated 11/9/1863, states:

To stock.

For amount of contract rebuilding chamber organ No 10162	£130/–/–
Making lowest octave of upper manual act on	
Bass of Great Organ	£2/–/–
An Organ Stool in Oak stuffed with horsehair &	
covered with Morocco leather	£7/13/3
Taking down Organ, travelling, re-erecting at Bleasby	£9/14/2
152 ft packing @ 8d	£5/1/4
Carriage	£5/12/5

MICHAEL J KEAYS

The organ at St Mary the Virgin, Bleasby, Notts, 2002

Rev John William Marsh was vicar of Bleasby Church from 1848 to 1875, and instigated renovations in that church in 1869 (which were also supported by a number of parishioners from Aylesford), the same year in which he gave the vicarage organ to the church.

The move from Bleasby Vicarage to the church is recorded in the Gray & Davison Ledger 8A page 315, where the organ is shown as being "taken down and moved" (not 'removed').

All this is further confirmed in the 1897 history of the Bleasby Parish, by Rev Henry L Williams (Vicar of Bleasby from 1888): "During his incumbency, Mr Marsh did excellent work, and was much beloved … [he] gave the sweet-toned organ which still leads the music in the church…". Barbara Cast records in *"The Church of Saint Mary's, Bleasby, Nottinghamshire" (1988/92):* "The fine and newly restored organ was given by Rev. Marsh and his family … After five moves around the country it was finally installed in Saint Mary's … where it enriches in tone and decoration our tiny church." The "Bleasby Terrier" (church inventory), provided in 2002 by Brian Temperley (then churchwarden at St Mary's Bleasby) & Diana Temperley confirms this: "Manual organ, electrically blown, in a fine carved case, given by The Revd. J.W.Marsh in 1869, it having been built for his grandfather in 1783."

The organ at St Mary's Bleasby was renovated, as noted by Barbara Cast, in the late 1980s: The Log Book of St Mary's Church records: "October 1986 organ rebuilt by Cousans Organs Lincoln, £6,935; January 1988 Organ casing decorated Dixon's of Southwell £477.25; June 1988 Exchanged organ blower with Halloughton (£160), Organ Tuning Cousans of Lincoln (£36)."

The specification of the organ is:

Upper manual		
Oboe	8 feet	
Principal	4 feet	
Leiblich Gedackt	8 feet	
Open Diapason	8 feet	

Lower manual		
Sesquialtera	2 rks	
Fifteenth	2 feet	
Principal	4 feet	
Clarabella	8 feet	
Stopt Diapason Bass	8 feet	
Clarinet Flute	8 feet	
Keraulophon	8 feet	
Open Diapason	8 feet	

Couplers
Upper manual to Lower
Lower manuals to Pedals

Accessories
Tremulant
3 combination pedals
Swell lever (2 notches)

Compass	
Manuals:	54 notes
Pedals:	2 octaves

The organ which was built for the composer John Marsh, and was in Aylesford Vicarage from 1840 until 1862, remains in use in Bleasby Church in 2015, some 232 years after it was built, which is a testament to the longevity of a well-maintained pipe organ. The author had the pleasure of playing this organ one very wet afternoon in 2002, thanks to Brian and Diana Temperley: With its historic links to Aylesford, this seemed entirely appropriate for the current organist of Aylesford.

Vicars of Aylesford in the Victorian era

The connection with the parish of St Mary the Virgin Bleasby, Notts., is much stronger than just that of an organ.

It is first worth reviewing the wider ecclesiastical organisation at the time. The Archdeaconry of Nottingham (including Southwell) was until 1837 in the Diocese of York, moving to the Diocese of Lincoln that year, and thus from the Province of York to the Province of Canterbury.

Rev Edward Garrard Marsh (1783-1862), vicar of Aylesford from 1840 until his death in July 1862 (at the age of 79), became a Residentiary Canon of Southwell, and on 2/8/1821, Prebendary of Woodborough *(Fosters' "Index Ecclesiasticus")*. Both Bleasby and Woodborough are north west of Nottingham, towards Southwell. Rev E G Marsh was a son of the composer John Marsh, and married Lydia Williams at Southwell in July 1813. They produced a large family, including John William Marsh (eldest son, c.1822) and Anne Caroline Marsh (daughter, c.1821).

John William Marsh became the vicar of St Mary's Bleasby, a parish just a few miles away from Woodborough, in 1848. At the time of the 1851 Census, he is recorded as being vicar of Bleasby and living with his sister, Anne Caroline Marsh (aged 29 and 30 respectively).

Anne clearly visited her parents in Aylesford regularly, and in so doing met Thomas Abbott, whom she married in January 1856. Thomas Abbott's father (also Thomas Abbott, deceased 1861) was churchwarden for a number of years, as was his wife (noted in vestry meeting minutes from March 1829).

Anne Caroline Marsh, then, is the daughter of the vicar, Rev E G Marsh, and the Mrs Abbott who in 1865 paid for the new organ at Aylesford.

A partial family tree of the Marsh family has been constructed by the author from the current evidence available, and is shown in Appendix H.

Rev E G Marsh wrote a number of theological works, including a "Metrical Translation of the Book of Psalms" in 1832 (which sold for 12s), and, whilst at Aylesford, "Seven Essays on Prophecies of Scripture not yet fulfilled" (1844-45, selling for 1s each).

Rev E G Marsh was also Bampton lecturer at Oxford University in 1848, with the subject "The Christian Doctrine of Sanctification"; his successor, The Rev Anthony Grant (vicar from 1862-1878) had been Bampton lecturer in 1843, with the subject "The Past and Prospective Extension of the Gospel by Missions to the Heathen".

In the 1871 Census, Rev Anthony Grant is listed as an occupant of the vicarage with, amongst others, his son Cyril Fletcher Grant, who later succeeded him as vicar of Aylesford (1878-1895), having been Curate for his Father between 1876 and 1878.

Rev Cyril Grant was succeeded by Rev George Vaux in 1895. The section on "Organists and Assistant Organists" describes events during his incumbency in more detail, although it is interesting to note that the UK Clergy List 1897 shows Rev Vaux serving his curacy in Wolverhampton, then as vicar of Christ Church, Tettenhall Wood, Wolverhampton, from 1885-1889: Co-incidentally, the author himself also spent many years in Tettenhall, Wolverhampton before moving to Aylesford.

A complete listing of the vicars of Aylesford from 1840 is produced in Appendix G.

ALL 14 PHOTOGRAPHS OF AYLESFORD VICARS, AYLESFORD CHURCH OFFICE

Rev Edward Garrard Marsh (1840-1862)

Rev Anthony Grant (1862-1877)

Rev Cyril Fletcher Grant (1878-1895)

Rev George Vaux (1895-1902)

Vicars of Aylesford 1902–present

Rev Arthur Thorndike (1902-1909)

Rev Thomas Sopwith (1909-1915)

Canon Frederick Everett (1915-1941)

Rev Trevor Southgate (1941-1950)

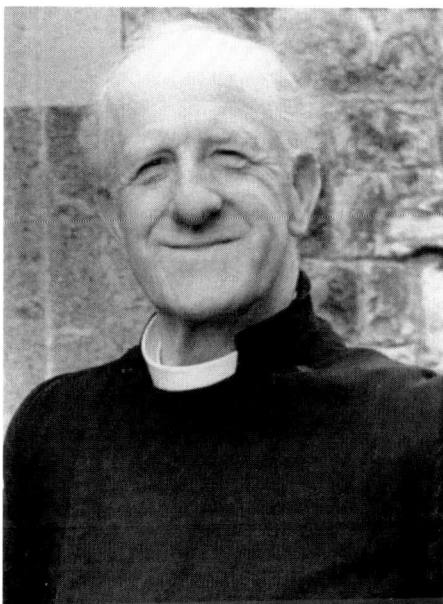

Canon Henry Powell (1950-1964)

Rev Alec Goodrich (1964-1980)

Rev Arthur Heathcote (1980-1990)

Rev Paul Francis (1990-2000)
left (with Rev Kevin Crinks, curate)

Rev Simon Tillotson (2000-2007)

Rev Chris van Straaten (2007-)

Betts and Brassey, Aylesford benefactors

In Victorian times, Aylesford was a very close-knit community, a rural parish: The church and school benefitted from the generosity of the owners of Preston Hall, who also provided the use of the Deer Park (the area immediately behind and to the east of Preston Hall, including the area now occupied by the Heart of Kent Hospice and Gavin Astor House) for school 'treats'. Church and school were also closely linked, with some Masters also being organists of the church. Aylesford was, as many villages of the time, largely self-sufficient, with a dairy and brewery, education and entertainment, and care for the poor.

For Aylesford, the latter half of the nineteenth century was something of a golden age. "In conjunction with the Squire the vicar ruled the village with autocratic paternalism" *(Powell, "Aylesford")*: "An Aylesford Squirearchy was predominantly exercised from Preston Hall."

In particular, the role played by Betts and Brassey, successive owners of nearby Preston Hall, is most significant. Some excellent studies exist on Preston Hall and its owners (Ken Wells' book of the same title is only available in manuscript, Jim Sephton's "Preston Hall, Aylesford" provides excellent background information, and uses Ken Wells' book as one of his sources); however, a brief summary of their influence on Aylesford Church is appropriate, not least because the history of the organ is very much tied-up with restorations to the church and the vast sums of money expended by these two Victorian philanthropists on church and organ, and indeed the village as a whole.

Edward Ladd Betts (1815-1872)
Preston Hall, 1848–1867

Betts was a successful railway builder, responsible (from 1848 in conjunction with Samuel Morton Peto (1809-1889)) for a number of major railway engineering projects, including the extension of the South Eastern Railway from Maidstone to Strood in 1856: This ran through the Preston Hall estate, and included the building of Aylesford station (opened on 18/6/1856), which has an architectural grandeur unlike other stations on the line. The financial schemes used by Peto and Betts to fund railway construction, though, were responsible for Betts' bankruptcy during the banking crisis of 1866, which forced him to sell Preston Hall in 1867 to Thomas Brassey (1805-1870), with whom Peto and Betts had previously worked from time to time.

RAY STURGEON COLLECTION

Aylesford Infants School, built 1853 (known as Preston Hall Infants School in 1868)

Betts was popular with the villagers. Amongst other things, he provided fresh water piped from springs at Tottington, built the school by the old bridge in 1853 (now The Brassey Centre) and the Wesleyan Chapel in Rochester Road. His departure from the village was recorded by the Maidstone Telegraph: "We should not forgive ourselves if we allowed you to depart from us without our expressing to you our deepfelt gratitude for the many benefits you have conferred upon this village." *(9/3/1867)*

Henry Arthur Brassey (1840-1891)
Preston Hall, 1870–1891

The second surviving son of the railway entrepreneur Thomas Brassey, HA Brassey was gifted Preston Hall by his Father, who had purchased it in 1867 when E L Betts' business interests failed.

Henry Arthur Brassey moved into Preston Hall on the death of his father, in 1870. HA Brassey's "first time of his meeting the public of Aylesford" was on Wednesday 5/10/1870 *(PM, November 1870)*. Until his death in 1891, he funded a number of major projects in the village, from the restoration of the church in 1878-9 (which included the moving and enlarging of the organ) and the restoration of the tower and bells in 1885. He also extended the school in Mount Pleasant: He was clearly a successful and wealthy businessman (he left £1.045m in his will), and the village benefitted greatly from his generosity.

HA Brassey was also Liberal MP for Sandwich from 1868 until 1885. His widow, Anna Brassey, and son Henry Leonard Brassey, were responsible for the 1892 extension to the Almshouses (Hospital of the Holy Trinity).

Henry's son, Henry Leonard, inherited Preston Hall in 1898 after the death of his mother. H L Brassey's wife, Violet, was the daughter of the 7th Duke of Richmond, and disliked what she considered the "faux aristocracy" associated with Preston Hall, stating that it was "only fit for commoners as it had no historical legacy". Accordingly, the Brassey family moved away (to Apelthorpe, in Northamptonshire) in 1904, and with that, the golden era closed.

However, the influence of the Brassey's did not end there: The Brassey Trust was set-up on 1/7/1905 by Henry Leonard Brassey, "to perpetuate the memory of his family who resided at Preston Hall … for 40 years … benefitting the … Parish by promoting the work of the Church of England". *(PM, October 1968, quoting from "The Instrument of the Brassey Trust")*. The Brassey Trust continues to support Aylesford Church, and in particular has made grants towards periodic work to maintain the viability of the organ and other aspects of the music ministry at Aylesford church.

Aylesford Church restorations in the Victorian era

During the Victorian era, and shortly thereafter, a number of changes and restorations were made to the interior of Aylesford Church: Over the one hundred years until the early 20th century, the appearance of the church changed beyond recognition. A gallery was built and removed; the west arch was blocked-up, then re-opened; the organ appeared in the west end of the church, then was moved to the east end; the vestry was built, then extended; the ceiling was removed to reveal the roof rafters; the west window was glazed with stained glass to become the massive Brassey Memorial window. The focus of worship moved to the south aisle, although the pulpit remained in the north aisle until after the fabric report of 1943, where it is described as being "in an awkward position"; the report recommended "its removal to the southern side of the nave, involving the removal of the front pew on this side".

Some of the work during the 19th century was a response to the growth in the population, other work was undertaken both to restore and preserve the church and to bring it into line with modern worship practices. The work was increasingly financed by the generosity of wealthy landowners, as previously noted.

First of all, it is worth considering Aylesford's population growth, which from 1811 to 1901 is listed in the vestry minute book 1736-1916, and for 1901 also in the Kent Messenger Directory of Maidstone 1904 *(KM)*: Details are provided in Appendix J. From a total population of 875 in 1811, the population had swelled to 2,937 by 1891 (despite some emigrations to Australia in the mid to late 1840s), easing back to 2,673 *(KM)* or 2,678 *(vestry minutes)* ten years later. (For reference, Aylesford's population was estimated as 6,078 in mid-1963; by 2011 the population of the civil parish of Aylesford was 10,660). The vestry meeting minutes of 18/5/1838 noted that alterations were needed to the pews in the body of the church, as there was insufficient accommodation for the Parishioners. The alterations required to accommodate a rising church membership also entailed the construction of a west end gallery, of which much more in the next section.

A new vestry was constructed in 1851 (now the choir vestry); as noted by Ken Wells to the author in 1988, the (clergy) vestry had previously been in the small tower on the south wall, with a robing pew leading from it; this small tower (which still exists behind the pulpit) provided access to the Rood Screen until the Reformation. The vestry was also the venue for vestry meetings, at least during the 1860s.

The dominant style of worship in the early 19th century was based around the Word, with the Cranmerian services of Matins and Evensong at either end of each Sunday's worship in Anglican churches across the land. Communion was generally only taken on Feast Days (Easter, Christmas etc), and then by less than 2% of Parishioners. As the 19th century progressed, the Church of England underwent various reforms, including the setting-up of schools (generally funded by the local gentry), missionary outreach (including massive church building programmes in England), and changes to worship. These latter changes were influenced primarily by the Tractarians, who became better known as the Oxford Movement: They argued that the church had become too "plain", and sought to re-establish reserve and sobriety in worship, advocating moving the centrality of preaching in worship to the sacrament of the Eucharist. Many church restorations were also strongly influenced by the ideals of the Oxford Movement, including enlarging chancels to accommodate the associated ritual, opening-up aisles to give a better view of the altar, removing box pews and galleries, and implementing elaborate decorative schemes throughout the church. Indeed, in the Aylesford vestry meeting minutes of 3/12/1868, the need was noted "to make some alterations in the chancel of the Parish Church"; and in the 1878-9 alterations (as noted below) more elements of this 'modernising' approach were undertaken in such changes as the decorations of the church walls (especially in the chancel) and by the robing of the choir.

In 1866, Aylesford church choir was formed. Once they had become established, permanent choir stalls were installed in the chancel as part of the 1878-9 renovation works (which also included the move of the organ to the east end of the church, closer to the choir): "The stall end nearest the Colepepper monument is ancient, and is one of the old priest stall ends" *(PM, October 1951)*. A sketch of the chancel pre-1852 shows one of these stall ends on the Preston Hall family pew.

This restoration, which cost around £3,500, was funded by HA Brassey, MP, of nearby Preston Hall: The vestry meeting minutes of 7/3/1878 discuss the "reception of Mr HA Brassey's offer to fund the necessary church renovations", which are noted as complete in the minutes of the 1/4/1879 Meeting. The vestry minutes of 14/4/1879 note:

> It was also resolved that the ratepayers of Aylesford in vestry assembled desire to express their sense of the great and lasting benefit conferred on the Parish by the Restoration of the Parish Church and to record their gratitude to Henry A Brassey Esq MP for having so generously undertaken the expense of so important a work.

AYLESFORD CHURCH OFFICE

Aylesford Church interior pre-1852 re-ordering. Note the undecorated North Chancel east window (now dedicated to the Earls of Aylesford and their wives) of what is now the Lady Chapel, and the door leading to the Preston Hall family pew (foreground left)

Ken Wells *(letters)* states that in this restoration plaster ceilings were removed, the west end arch re-opened, gallery removed, and the organ moved to the chancel aisle (the move actually took place early in 1879). To accommodate the new position of the organ, it is likely that at this point the font was moved from chancel aisle to under the tower, and a new pulpit installed in the north aisle (photographic evidence from around 1900 shows this still in the north aisle); further 1878 works included the installation of gas lighting and the rebuilding of south and west porches.

Photographs exist from 1879, showing the temporary position of the organ in the North Aisle Chancel (now the Lady Chapel) and its final position from November 1879, once enlarged. These photographs also prove conclusively that the church interior was not decorated until the final part of the restoration, which included the organ enlargement, decoration and move, in November 1879, although the altar frontal with the Latin "Ego sum panis vitae" ("I am the bread of life") is present on all of these photographs.

From November 1879 the interior walls of the church were decorated in typical high Victorian Gothic revival style, with the decoration of the organ case pipework undertaken by Forster and Andrews designed to fit the overall scheme within the church: Photographs from the late 19th century show stencilled walls and a highly elaborate east wall behind the altar, both of which had been plain (as now) prior to late 1879.

The liturgy of Aylesford church, possibly encouraged by the liturgy and ritual of Rochester Cathedral, moved progressively more in line with the views of the Oxford Movement: This culminated in a stand-off between the vicar and some of the congregation in 1900, when liturgical practices came to a head during the incumbency of Rev George Vaux, as described in more detail in the section "Organists and Assistant Organists", below.

The newly-glazed west window was unveiled as the Brassey Memorial window on 27/10/1892 *(PM, November 1892)*; the final part of the reordering of the church occurred in 1908, with an extension of the new (clergy) vestry: The old entrance (which had been under the gallery) was blocked-up, and the former north door of the church used to provide access to the enlarged vestry.

PRESTON HALL COLLECTION

Aylesford church interior, with stencilled walls, pulpit in north aisle, and organ in the North Aisle Chapel (now the Lady Chapel). c.1900

View of the organ in the North Aisle Chapel (now the Lady Chapel), clearly showing the arrangements of the (completed) panels, thus later than 1907

The west end gallery

It is well documented that there was once a gallery against the west end wall of the church, and that it was accessed from the west door by means of a staircase through the west end arch, at that time blocked-off. What is less clear is exactly what size this gallery was.

Detailed observations, measurements and photographs undertaken early in 2015 by the author have now shed some light on the construction and size of the gallery. Unfortunately, there is no photographic or sketch evidence of the gallery from the time, although some traces of it can still be seen in repairs to the masonry of the central west wall pillar, and the pillar immediately to the east of this one. Those in the west wall pillar are large enough to suggest they once held support timbers; those in the next pillar are quite small, and slightly higher, suggesting that at most they supported a guard rail or gallery front. There are no markings on the west end arch, which appears to have been completely restored, rather than patched, in the 1878-9 restoration when the gallery was removed. It is almost certain that the gallery remained in place until early 1879: The organ was temporarily positioned in the North Aisle Chancel (now the Lady Chapel)

in February 1879, prior to major works at the end of 1879, and there is no recorded evidence of works to move the organ over the previous 12 months.

From documentary evidence, the gallery accommodated both parishioners and the organ, which provides the first clue as to how deep it was built, a further clue being observed from masonry repairs to two of the pillars at the height of the gallery. Indeed, the height of the gallery is able to be determined from both observation (masonry repairs on the pillars) and historical documentation from 1851 *(vestry meeting minutes)* outlining the construction of a new vestry with a door "under the gallery", which would need to fit fully beneath the gallery floor. This latter piece of evidence also confirms the northern limit of the gallery.

The southern limit of the gallery is rather more open to conjecture. Against a gallery running the full length of the west wall (as Ken Wells suggests) is the fact that the south window is low, and thus would be intersected by the edge of the gallery. However, even in 1851, as shown in a sketch of the north west corner of the outside of the church by E Pretty, there was a matching window in the north wall, which was in existence when the gallery was built some 13 years earlier. This north wall window would also have been intersected by the edge of the gallery. High on the north wall (inside church), beyond the north door and near the junction with the west wall, it is possible to see traces of the top of this old window. This window was almost certainly blocked-up when the new vestry was built on the north side of the church (and a doorway inserted below the old window, now also blocked-up), in 1851. From the 1851 sketch by E Pretty, it is also possible to determine that the west window design remained unaltered when glazed as

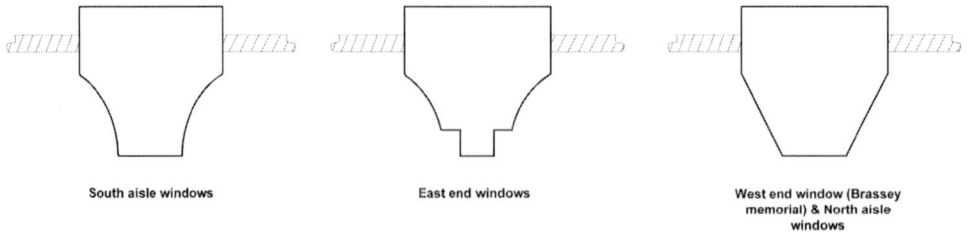

| South aisle windows | East end windows | West end window (Brassey memorial) & North aisle windows |

Sketches of the window mullions at Aylesford Church

the Brassey Memorial Window in 1892; the lower lights of this window appear to be filled with masonry in 1851, which is consistent with a gallery running across it at this level.

The other two possibilities of the southern extent of the gallery are that it was in line with the south edge of the west arch, or that it was in line with the edge of the door providing access to the gallery through the blocked-up west arch. No drawings or photographs exist to confirm the actual layout, although a full-length gallery appears to be the most logical, despite the impact on the south and north wall windows. Detailed scale drawings (see next page) clarify the findings.

Further evidence that the west window was in existence, and largely unaltered in its design and tracery, prior to 1892, comes from newspaper reports at the time of the unveiling of the Brassey Memorial window *(Sussex Agricultural Express, 29/10/1892)*: Whilst the mullions suggest that the current window tracery is of a later vintage than the windows in the south wall, and less ornate, there are similarities in overall design between the two when compared with other windows in the church (for example, the window arch is steeper than the frame within which it sits). It is almost certain that the window was restored when it was filled with stained glass in 1892, to create the Brassey Memorial window. The original west window would have been completely obscured between 1865 and early 1879 when the organ was in its gallery position, making the church quite gloomy at dusk.

The vestry meeting minutes dated 18/5/1838 describe the 1838 restoration of Aylesford Church, which was mainly to accommodate more parishioners (with an increase in the number of pews). They also mention the (west end) gallery with seating accommodation for larger children, and seating accommodation for the infants underneath. A staircase ran from the west door to the gallery, and the west end arch was filled with masonry. The font was then in the North Chancel (near the Culpepper monument), rather than close to the tower as now (moved from under the tower in 2009), and the pulpit, reading desk and clerk's desk were in the north aisle, that being the main area of the church used for the liturgy during the Victorian era. It is almost certain that there was never a village 'gallery band' in Aylesford – the gallery came far too late – and indeed by the time the gallery was built, a barrel organ had been purchased (in 1838) for the leading of the worship, and this was installed in the gallery, in the position to be occupied nearly 30 years later by the new organ.

LIKELY POSITION OF THE GALLERY & 1865 ORGAN IN AYLESFORD CHURCH, KENT

N

WEST END OF CHURCH

West end arch
12' 11" (3.94m)

Brassey memorial window
9' 8" (2.96m)

Blocked-up door
2' 4" (0.72m)

Former North window

3' 4" (1.02m)

6' 8" (2.03m)

1865 F&A ORGAN
Original position

Line of front of organ

10' 6" (3.2m)

North door

A

6' 8" (2.03m)

Probable extent of front of gallery

a   1' 6" (0.46m)
b   2' 4" (0.72m)

a

4' 5" (1.35m)

Likely position of access stairway / door

13' 5" (4.10m)

b

B

Possible extent of south side of gallery (3 potential positions)

2' 10" (0.56m)

Window
6' 9" (2.67m)

4' (1.23m)

South door

4' 6" (1.37m)

Gallery depth: 13' 5" (4.10m)

Gallery width: 36' 6" (11.16m)   OR   41' 10" (12.77m)   OR   46' 4" (14.14m)

CENTRAL PILLARS

■ Evidence of masonry repairs

Pillar A, looking West

West wall

Pillar B, looking East

WEST WALL, NORTH END

West end arch

A

Most likely height of gallery

Height to bottom of South window
5' 3" (1.61m)

NORTH WALL, WEST END

North door

Trace of former North window

8'
(2.44m)

Blocked-up door

7' 6"
(2.24m)

1865 F&A ORGAN
Original position

Brassey memorial window

[Installed in 1892, after removal of gallery. Original window dimensions appear from an 1851 sketch to have been identical]

The following summary of the gallery can be determined with some degree of confidence:

The gallery:

- Was installed in 1838

- Had access via a staircase from the west door through a high-level opening in the blocked-up west arch

- Ran along the west wall, probably for its entire length, at 46' 4" (14.14m) (most likely), 41' 10" (12.77m) or 36' 6" (11.16m)

- Was built at a height of just under 8' (2.44m) above the floor, and to a depth of 13' (3.99m) as evidenced by high-level masonry repairs in the two west-most central pillars

- Was sturdy enough to support the weight of people and the organ

- Was illuminated initially by a window in the south wall, a window in the north wall and partially by a large window in the west wall (i.e. both sides and behind); in 1851, the north window was removed, and in 1865 the west window was blocked fully (by the new (and larger) organ) – progressively, the amount of natural light to the gallery reduced

- Was a flat surface, evidenced from the relative position of the masonry markings, to accommodate the organ without modification

- Accommodated the barrel organ as well as a harmonium (from 1863) and then, from 1865, the new organ (at 11' 3½" (3.43m) wide, smaller than the current instrument), in the north aisle gallery position in the centre (see left)

- Was removed early in 1879

The position of the organ from 1838 to 1878

There has been some debate on the original position of both the barrel organ and the 1865 Forster and Andrews organ for a number of years; in the first edition of this history, the author felt that on balance the Forster and Andrews organ had not been installed in the gallery, not least because the angels on top of the casework would have made the instrument too high to fit anywhere other than on the ground. David Wintle of NP Mander Ltd, observed in 1987 that the Great soundboard is unusually long and narrow, suggesting that the organ was built in the gallery. Ken Wells *(letters, 20/6/1986)* believed that the organ was removed to the North Aisle Chancel during the 1878 restoration, when the gallery was dismantled during the reordering of the interior of the church under the auspices of Henry Arthur Brassey, of nearby Preston Hall, but did not name the organ builder responsible for this work; Smetham *(Rambles, p.209)* stated that the organ "was first placed in the old gallery, where it took the place of the old barrel organ of 1838", again, giving nothing further to support this view. At the time of writing the first edition (1988), visual evidence appeared to overwhelmingly support an initial position in the Lady Chapel (North Aisle Chancel) rather than the gallery.

However, in the intervening years, more historic documentation has been discovered which points conclusively to a gallery position, at least for the first 13 years of the organ's life. Key amongst the discoveries has been the Forster & Andrews order book which details the purchase of the casework angels in 1879, and the significant widening of the organ at the same time, demonstrating conclusively that the organ was narrower and slightly lower in height in 1865 than now, and thus just able to be accommodated in a raised position in the gallery. It has also transpired that Forster and Andrews undertook two distinct pieces of work on the organ in 1879, with the second of which including the expansion of the organ, the decoration of the case pipework and the moving of the organ to the "North Wall of Aisle" (later referred to as the Lady Chapel).

Photographic evidence showing the organ in a position to the east of the North Aisle Chancel supports the 'move' of the organ in 1879, but does not rule-out an original gallery position; detailed measurements have concluded that this pre-north wall position (where the Lady Chapel altar is now positioned) can only have been a temporary expedient, to allow the dismantling of the gallery to proceed. The barrel organ would appear to have been installed in a central north aisle position in the gallery, where the replacement organ was to be built in 1865 *(Ken Wells, extrapolated from the Church Book of 1918, letters, 20/1/1988)*.

Certainty of the position of the 1865 organ is very much confirmed by the smaller dimensions of the original instrument, and we can be confident of where this was from scale drawings created as part of the research for this edition of the organ history.

The gallery would appear to have been flat, deep enough to accommodate the organ and provide adequate access across the front of the organ to reach all areas.

The organ was designed with case pipework displayed on three sides, thus not intended for any corner position. The back of the Swell box was solid and flat, and placed right at the back of the organ, thus the instrument needed a flat space behind it, and could not be placed against a pillar. The rear of the Swell box would have been directly against the wall and window: Even in its later position in the North Aisle Chancel (now Lady Chapel), the back of the Swell box would still have been flat against the wall and blocked-up windows. Maintenance access to the Swell box would have been solely from the front; the current rear access panels date from 1965, when the organ was moved, as noted below.

Additional space is also required at the sides of the organ, in particular on the right side of the organ (initially the north of the organ), in order to accommodate the organ blower and the blower lever. Further, the panel which contained the blower lever was also the means of maintenance access into the organ, as evidenced by the lock which can still be seen in the top centre of this panel.

Scale drawings indicate that the organ could only be accommodated in a central gallery position (south or north aisle) due to height constraints (a total height of approx. 8' (2.44m) plus 17' 2" (5.25m) for the organ). In the south aisle position, this would have blocked the west end arch, within which was set the gallery entrance doorway; with just 10" (0.25m) clearance either side of the west arch, this would have been insufficient to provide any gallery access at all.

Thus the only possible position for the organ was central in the north aisle gallery position, flat against the wall, in front of (and obscuring) the west window. This would create a good visual position for the organ, as well as allowing it to speak well into the church, in particular the north aisle.

Once the organ was installed, the only natural light would have come from the south window (and then only the upper part of it), so the gallery was not well lit.

The following summarises the position of the 1865 organ and can be verified with some degree of confidence from historical records, observations and scale drawings:

- The dimensions of the 1865 organ are able to be determined from those of the current organ, with the width of the 1865 instrument being just the section between the innermost casework pillars (with the console doors in the centre), i.e. 11' 3½" (3.43m) wide by 8' 5" (2.57m) deep (excluding cornices, which add a further 4" (0.10m) to the front and sides just above eye-level)

- The 1865 organ was installed in the gallery, as a replacement for the barrel organ and also a harmonium (installed in the church in 1863, presumably also in the gallery)

- The position of the 1865 organ is also the position of the barrel organ which it replaced

- The 1865 organ was installed in the north aisle gallery position in the centre (see gallery drawing above), blocking the west window (albeit well before the creation of the Brassey Memorial window in 1892, some time after the gallery had been removed) –

  o At the time, there were no angels on the case (which was considerably smaller): These appeared as part of the November 1879 organ works, which included moving it from the gallery to a temporary location (February 1879) and moving it to a permanent position, extending it (November 1879)

  o The main liturgical action at the time appears to have been centred around the north aisle, and a north aisle position for the organ would support this position of worship

- Co-incidentally, this west end centre north aisle position of the organ was the recommendation of Harold Moore in 1964, albeit in 1964 it would have been at ground-level rather than on a gallery: This position was only made unacceptable by the need to avoid obscuring the Brassey Memorial window, and thus the move in 1965 from the North Aisle Chancel was to its present position against the North Nave wall.

The decoration of the organ

The first impression of the organ that the visitor gains today is the impressive array of painted panelling (screening the bellows, blower, and some of the larger pipework), the decorated pipework, and the four gilded angels surmounting the organ, holding their trumpets, lyres and horns.

The panelling is of some great interest: The angels on these were hand-painted by a local lady who was thought previously (by the author and by Ken Wells *(letters, 20/6/1986)*) to have died before completing her work. New evidence has emerged which disproves this. The unfinished panels, when located in the organ's North Aisle Chancel position, would never have been seen. A photograph from around 1900, with the organ in the North Aisle Chancel, shows the half-completed panel partially hidden by the chancel arch, with all other painted panels on display on the west and south sides of the organ; by deduction, those on the east side would be the undecorated panels. In a similar manner, Forster & Andrews did not decorate the case pipework on the east side in 1879: both the panels and the pipes would be completely out of view, butting against the north aisle chancel altar and the Banks memorial.

Ken Wells says that 'There is very good evidence to suggest that the organ was decorated by Miss Edith Login, daughter of Lady Login of the Cedars, Aylesford ..." *(Letters, 12/4/1987)*: This view is supported by the vestry minutes of 1/4/1907 which acknowledge Miss Edith Login's "kindness in painting the panels in the screens of the Lady Chapel": The only screens were those around the organ, and the panels within them are those that have been painted. Miss Edith D Login continued to be present at vestry meetings until at least 5/4/1915, thus lived well beyond the completion of her work.

Ken Wells' own researches *(letters 17/1/1988)* confirm these facts on the decoration of the organ panels: "No doubt it was carried out c.1890 – c.1910", thus, starting around 1890 and completing in 1907 as noted above. Ken Wells correctly states that it was "done after the organ was sited in the North Aisle Chancel. It seems quite logical that only those parts which were visible from the nave should be decorated. As far as the north west part of the casing was concerned, this would have been partly obscured by the chancel arch and pillar and also the pulpit, which in those days was sited in the north east corner of the nave and backed up to the organ. The lectern was sited in the south east corner of the nave."

The overall decorative scheme of the organ (i.e. pipework and panels) was commenced in 1879 and complete in 1907; it is now the only reminder of the richness of the decoration that was present throughout the church in the late Victorian era, and still discernible from photographic evidence.

Set into the organ panelling was the original console, linked by trackers to the organ itself. The old sliding doors can still be seen in the middle, and were re-opened for the first time in nearly 50 years during the dismantling works for the 2015 restoration, in 2014. Above this is a carved wooden date plate, provided by Forster and Andrews during the 1879 rebuild, as noted later under the 1879 works.

Above the panelling are some decorated pipes on the west and south facing sides, and lightly stencilled pipes on the east facing side. The back half of the pipework on the two sides are non-speaking dummy pipes, and the remainder on these sides are part of the Pedal Open Diapason 16'. The pipes on the front outer flats (i.e. left and right of the central section of the front case pipes) are again dummy pipes, with the exception of one pipe on each side, which form part of the Pedal Principal 8'. The pipes between the two central pillars are all speaking pipes, being a mix of Great Open Diapason 8' and Great Dulciana 8'.

Above the front pipes are four gilded angels, each 3' (0.91m) in height, which by 2014 had become quite badly damaged. As part of the restoration works, these were removed from the organ and transported to Oad Street (their first trip outside the church in 135 years!), for repair and restoration by Nigel Wheeler, a specialist repairer, at a cost of £525. The repairs included light-touch re-gilding, so as not to stand-out too much against the decorated case pipework (which has not undergone restoration).

The dimensions of the organ are as follows:

Date	Height	Depth	Width	Notes
1865	17' 3" 5.25m	8' 5" 2.57m	11' 3½" 3.44m	
1879	19' 2" 5.84m	8' 5" 2.57m	16' 3" 4.96m	*Organ extended & angels added*
1965	19' 2" 5.84m	10' 5" 3.18m	16' 3" 4.96m	*Also extended rearwards into the window reveal*

Cornices, just above eye-level, add a further 4" (0.10m) to the organ dimensions on both sides and the front of the case.

Forster & Andrews, organ builders

This Hull firm commenced business in 1843, continuing until 1956 when they were taken over by the London firm of Hill, Norman and Beard Ltd. The 1865 organ at Aylesford was Order No 375, and thus one of the earlier of the 1,378 instruments constructed by them over their 113 year history: At the time of the construction of the instrument, the company had been established just 22 years.

James Alderson Forster and Joseph King Andrews met whilst they were both apprentices at J C Bishop, in London, working together in 1842 on alterations to the organ in Temple Church (which they rebuilt in 1878). There were many good reasons for setting-up business in Hull: Forster was born in Hull, which was also the 4th most important city in England at the time for commerce; there was also a plentiful supply of timber coming into Hull docks on the north side of the Humber estuary; there were also very few Northern-based organ builders. Thus in 1843 Forster & Andrews set-up the 'Organ Manufactory' in the old Mechanics Institute, 29 Charlotte Street, Hull (now George Street).

The railway between Hull and London had opened in 1840, enabling a link with London contacts to continue, and, more importantly, London was the major railway hub from which other parts of the country could be reached easily (particularly Kent, which was served well by both the South Eastern Railway (from 1842) and the London, Chatham and Dover Railway (from 1861)). Indeed, some 4% of Forster & Andrews' new organs were built in Kent, including instruments at St Paul's Chatham, St Margaret's Rochester (extended by FH Browne in 1902), All Saints Frindsbury, SS Peter & Paul Leybourne, St John's Mote Park, Maidstone, and at St George's Wrotham. They also carried out additions to the 1791 Samuel Green organ at Rochester Cathedral in 1876. Despite the advent of the railways, travel to country churches in Victorian times remained a limiting challenge, as noted from Forster & Andrews' order book relating to the 1877 build of the organ at St Mary the Virgin, Kemsing: "Kemsing: London, Chatham and Dover Railway – book to Kemsing; if train does not stop get out at Otford Junction and walk two miles": Whilst these instructions date from five years before Otford Station opened, to replace the earlier junction exchange platform, the lack of a regular service to Kemsing is still true to this day!

The instrument at Aylesford was one of the first they constructed in the county: A comprehensive listing of organs built or altered by Forster & Andrews in Kent is included in Appendix B.

Just eight years after commencing business, the 1851 Great Exhibition took place in Crystal Place, London: Prince Albert (of Saxe-Coburg) invited Schulze, the German organ builder, to exhibit one of his organs (Edmund Schulze came from the Thuringia area of Germany, as (a few years earlier) did J S Bach). The opportunity to exhibit in England, with a Royal invitation, was enough to popularise Schulze organs in England; one of the best examples of their work is still in existence in St Bartholomew's Church, Armley, Leeds. In the February 2002 edition of the 'Organist's Review', Paul Hale (Organist at Southwell Minster and formerly Diocesan Organ Adviser in the Rochester Diocese) noted that, "A firm particularly inspired by Schulze was Forster & Andrews of Hull. They were early in developing factory methods of production which resulted in colossal output through the 1870s, 80s and 90s ... their excellent voicing, large scales and fine wooden basses proclaimed them to be progressive disciples of Schulze's work ...": Forster & Andrews also exhibited at the Great Exhibition of 1851, and clearly realised that there was a good market in producing organs with similarities to Schulze's: Edmund Schulze, as noted by Nicholas Thistlewaite, would also recommend Forster & Andrews to prospective clients when he was unable to accept commissions. As Frank Fowler noted (Quotation to Aylesford on behalf of Hill, Norman & Beard Ltd) in 1986, "the organ [at Aylesford] is of excellent pedigree."

By the late 1850s, the company employed nearly 30 people, and ten years later, around 30 new organs were built by them every year (including the one at Aylesford) – an average of more than one new organ every fortnight! Forster & Andrews prided themselves on manufacturing organs at 20% lower than London prices, and on durability well in excess of 50 years – a claim which at Aylesford time has proven to be well justified!

Forster & Andrews organs were always "well and solidly built" (Sumner 'The Organ', page 245); they were very solidly constructed, employing all available accessories and many innovations. They experimented with a transposing organ between 1847 and 1849, but their innovations really flourished at the turn of the 19th and 20th century under the direction of Philip H Selfe: The specification of the organ at Hull City Hall (organ built in 1911) controversially included Drums, Tubular Bells and Steel Bars, a specification fast approaching one that might come from the workshops of Compton in England, or

Wurlitzer in America, a few years later! For the organ enthusiasts, this instrument also contains an acoustic 64' Pedal stop (Gravissima).

The period 1870-1900 is considered by Laurence Elvin to be the best period of Forster and Andrews' tonal developments: The bulk of the work at Aylesford was immediately prior to this, although the significant extension of the organ in 1879 falls comfortably within this period, and supports this comment; the strong tonal quality of the organ at Aylesford compares favourably with much of the work of more established organ builders (e.g. Willis). This period was also one of major production output, with a very impressive list of organs built or altered during these years: The Hull History Centre Archive lists the contents of their Ledgers, and this runs for very many pages.

Laurence Elvin wrote an excellent and detailed book on Forster and Andrews' work entitled 'Forster and Andrews Organ Builders, 1843-1956': it is strongly recommended that this is read, although it is unfortunately currently out of print.

Part 2: 1865–1965

The inauguration of the new Forster & Andrews organ *(1865)*

No records exist of how the new organ was selected, how the specification was agreed, or indeed why the Hull firm of Forster & Andrews were chosen to undertake the work.

Despite the date of '1879' on the organ case, it is well documented that the inauguration of the new Forster & Andrews organ was in 1865, the same year in which the Parish Magazine was first published: In the January 1866 edition, under the heading "Church Notes", the following appears:

> The New Organ, which has been presented to the church by the munificence of Mrs Abbot [*sic*], was publicly opened on Friday, Dec. 8th. There was full Evening Service at 3.30pm, after which an eloquent Sermon was preached by the Lord Bishop of Rochester. Mr Hopkins, organist of Rochester Cathedral, presided at the organ, and the whole of the Cathedral Choir also lent their valuable services. There was a very large congregation, who must have thoroughly enjoyed the beautiful singing and chanting of such a superior choir. The organ was built by the eminent firm of Forster and Andrews, of Hull, at a cost of £270. It consists of two manuals, CC to G, and a pedal organ, and is considered by competent judges to be an excellent instrument both for power and sweetness of tone.

The Maidstone and Kentish Journal of 4/12/1865 and 11/12/1865 contained reports of the new organ, also stating that a collection of £13 had been raised at the opening service to help defray "certain expenses connected with the erection of the instrument". No other record exists of these additional costs, or indeed whether the £13 raised covered them completely.

The Bishop's sermon for the opening service is quoted at length in both the Maidstone and Kentish Journal *(11/12/1865)* and the Maidstone Telegraph and West Kent Messenger *(16/12/1865)*. The following extract is representative of the whole:

Let then the full-toned swell of the organ be heard amidst the noble architecture of that house ... let the majestic solemnity and sweetness of their [i.e. the pipes] sound lead them [i.e. the people] to a devout and holy frame of mind, and abstract their hearts from the things of the world, and raise up their thoughts in heavenly aspirations, ... for the earnest heartfelt praise of the living God.

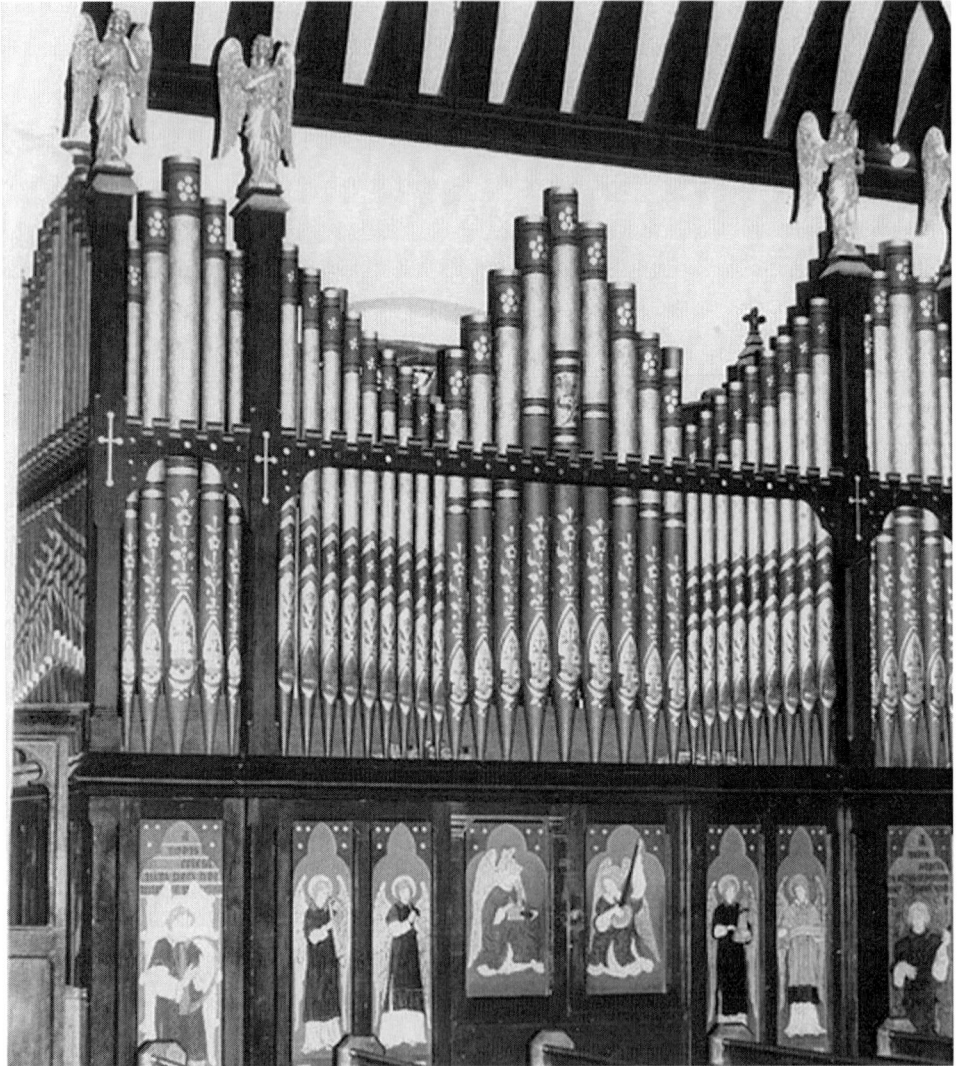

The Forster & Andrews organ case, Aylesford church, 1988

Although the Swell division consisted of seven ranks of pipes, only two of these had the full compass of a 56 note range, with the remainder being built to Tenor C only, although two of the ranks were "prepared to CC" (i.e. to allow the bottom octave to be added later), and a further rank (The Flûte d'Amour 8') was "grooved" to the Stopt Diapason 8', i.e. borrowed its bottom octave from the Stopt Diapason rank. This was common practice in Victorian organ building, both for reasons of economy (the bass pipes being the largest and most expensive) and space (the Swell box being the constraining factor).

Some registration aids were provided on the original instrument: Three mechanical combination pedal levers were added, to control pre-set stop selection. These were replaced by switch programmable thumb combination pistons in the 1965 rebuild, and by electronically controlled thumb and toe pistons in 2015.

The build date of 1865 was further confirmed during the 1965 rebuild, when the signature "A Hall, 1865" was found by Manders in the Swell soundboard *(NP Mander letter to Harold Moore, 6/4/1965)*.

The organ was built as a tracker-action organ and was hand-pumped. According to the National Pipe Organ Register (NPOR) ref. N14700, the pedalboard was flat and straight, and the console stop knob font was Old English: Both of these are highly likely, particularly as the pedalboard was replaced in November 1879 (and again in 1965). The organ is shown in the Forster & Andrews order book as "No 375". The Forster and Andrews order book and ledger make for interesting reading:

- Firstly, the order book (page 102) gives the opening date as follows: "Opened by Mr Hopkins Dec 1. 1865": This is likely to have been the date on which the organ was handed-over to the church; the opening recital was definitely on the following Friday (8th December), as confirmed by documentary evidence from the time.

- The total cost of the organ was "£270 Nett". Ledger entry 338, which relates to this build, also shows the receipt of £271/1/0 on 12/12/1865 (i.e. payment in full at the end of the job), with the word "Carriage" most likely indicating the additional guinea (£1 1s) as being the transaction costs. What is also shown is "Com. to Mr J Hopkins, Rochester, £20", presumably the commission due to the cathedral organist (also mentioned in the order book) for advice on the build, and possibly even the recommendation of Forster and Andrews.

- The actual cost of the organ, then, was £250, plus £20 commission (£270 in total): Forster & Andrews order book notes show that the £270 was paid as follows: 'Mrs Abbott ordered to £250, Mrs Grant, Aylesford Vicarage, £20' (see the section "Vicars of Aylesford in the mid-Victorian era" (above) concerning Mrs Abbott and Mrs Grant).

- A further cost of at least £13 was incurred for unspecified expenses connected with the erection of the new organ.

- There is an interesting error in the order book (also copied across to the ledger at a later stage), where the Swell pipe count is shown as 308 pipes, but the total of the individual ranks (as detailed by Forster & Andrews) is actually 332.

The benefactors of the organ were both related to Aylesford vicars. Mrs Abbott was the daughter of Rev Edward Marsh, the previous vicar, and had married into the Abbott family, active members of Aylesford church; Mrs Grant was the wife of the then vicar, Rev Anthony Grant.

1865 SPECIFICATION
Forster & Andrews

Compass:　　Manuals CC - g3, 56 note.
Pedals CCC - C, 25 note.
Tracker Action, 3" wind.

Great		**Swell** (enclosed)	
1. Open Diapason	8'	9. Lieblich Bourdon (TC)	16'
2. Dulciana	8'	10. Open Diapason	8'
3. Stopt Diapason	8'	(TC, prepared to CC)	
4. Principal	4'	11. Stopt. Diapason	8'
5. Flauto traverso	4'	12. Flûte d'Amour	8'
6. Twelfth	2 ⅔'	(TC, CC-BB from No 11)	
7. Fifteenth	2'	13. Principal	4'
8. Mixture	III	14. Cornopean	8'
		(TC, prepared to CC)	
Pedal		15. Oboe (TC)	8'
16. Bourdon	16'		

Accessories
17. Swell to Great coupler
18. Great to Pedals coupler
19. 3 combination pedals
20. Trigger Swell pedal

(917 pipes)

Notes:
F&A incorrectly totalled Swell pipes as 308 instead of 332.
8 - Composition unknown, but most likely 15.19.22.
Swell initially built mainly to Tenor C (TC), with bottom octave prepared.

55

Move and enlargement of the Forster & Andrews organ *(1879)*

Major refurbishment, funded by HA Brassey, was carried out in the church in 1878-9; as a part of this two separate pieces of work were undertaken on the organ by Forster & Andrews during 1879, shown in their "Repairs and Additions" order book, pages 98 and 99 respectively.

The west end gallery was removed early in 1879, as soon as the organ was moved: The organ was temporarily relocated (part of the first changes to the organ, completed in February 1879) in the North Aisle Chancel (Lady Chapel), beneath the east window (in between the Banks and Culpepper memorials), as shown in a photograph from that time. The width available between the two memorials is insufficient to accommodate the organ (at its original 11' 3½" (3.44m) width) against the east wall, immediately under the chancel window, thus the temporary position is most likely to have been in the middle of the raised area, with the front of the instrument sufficiently far away from the altar step to allow space for the pedalboard, organ bench and organist, and space at the side for the organ blower.

The work completed early in 1879 comprised the addition of a new Pedal stop (Open Diapason 16', with a bottom octave of wood, which gave rise to the renaming of the entire rank as "Open Wood" in 1965 (reversed in 2015)), a Swell to Pedal coupler, and new bellows (to provide enough wind for the new pedal stop). Mentioned on the order book are Rev Cyril Grant, HA Brassey MP (Preston Hall), and H Woolley "Prof. Music". The cost of these works was £95.

(See over for the specification from February 1879.)

The second piece of work in 1879, commissioned only four months later, was considerably more extensive, enlarging the organ both physically and tonally, in a new position against the north wall in the North Aisle Chancel (Lady Chapel).

The Forster & Andrews order book for the November 1879 works mention placing the organ "against the north wall of aisle": This is clearly the chancel, where the enlarged organ case was designed to utilise all the space available in the area against the north wall of the North Aisle Chancel.

FEBRUARY 1879 SPECIFICATION
Forster & Andrews

Compass: Manuals CC - g3, 56 note.
Pedals CCC - C, 25 note.
Tracker Action, 3" wind.

Great

1.	Open Diapason	8'
2.	Dulciana	8'
3.	Stopt Diapason	8'
4.	Principal	4'
5.	Flauto traverso	4'
6.	Twelfth	2⅔'
7.	Fifteenth	2'
8.	Mixture	III

Pedal

16.	Bourdon	16'
17.	Open Diapason	16'

Swell (enclosed)

9.	Lieblich Bourdon (TC)	16'
10.	Open Diapason	8'
	(TC, prepared to CC)	
11.	Stopt. Diapason	8'
12.	Flûte d'Amour	8'
	(TC, CC-BB from No 11)	
13.	Principal	4'
14.	Cornopean	8'
	(TC, prepared to CC)	
15.	Oboe (TC)	8'

Accessories
17. Swell to Great
18. Great to Pedals
19. 3 combination pedals
20. Trigger Swell pedal

(942 pipes)

Notes:
17 & 20 new.

The extended case (16' 3" (4.96m)) fitted tightly against the altar steps on the east side (allowing enough space between the organ and the Banks memorial for maintenance access through the locked panel, and for the organ blower and the blower lever). On the west side, the organ was placed tight against the chancel arch, obscuring some of the dummy pipework (thus with no material effect on the operation of the organ):

The current west side cornice has been extended from the protruding outer edge of the former rear pillar to the north wall, by Mander's, in 1965, suggesting that this piece of cornice was not present when the organ was in the North Aisle Chancel, and thus fitted tightly into the chancel arch. The rear of the organ was flat against the north wall, evidenced by a cut-out in the east side cornice, to accommodate the edge of the Milner memorial: Photographic evidence confirms these measurements, showing that only 5' 9" (1.77m) of the west side of the organ was visible to the right of the chancel arch.

In order to accommodate the organ, two of the north wall windows of the North Aisle Chancel (shown in the 1851 sketch of the church by E Pretty) had to be blocked-up. Although there is no mention of this in the vestry minutes, the subsequent unblocking of the windows in 1966, after the organ was moved once again, is evidence of this.

Whether there was a thought to reinstall the (extended) organ back against the west end wall of the church on completion of the restoration is unknown; what is known is that the organ remained in its temporary position for a few months until achieving its final position in the North Aisle Chancel in November 1879, where it remained until 1965.

The Forster & Andrews order book contains both 'official' text and some interesting pencilled notes, presumably made by their surveyor after the initial work had been commissioned. It is possible to decipher most of the handwritten notes, and the entire order book entry, totalling £131, merits reproduction:

> Order book entry, crossed through as "Opened .. Nov 1879" (it is unclear whether the actual date is the 1st or the 6th – respectively a Saturday or a Thursday):
> **Aylesford Church No 375. Ordered by HA Brassey, MP, 4th June 1879.**
> Alter the form of Organ and place it against the North wall of Aisle, shewing large wood pipes ornamented at end next Church, making instrument wider as shewn in tracing, with figures of Angels top of posts.

> | | |
> |---|---|
> | Without figurines | 87 - - |
> | Four figurines | 30 - - |
> | Low Oct Sw Bourdon | 14 - - |

> All the improvements would be enclosed, and have the appearance of being a portion of the original Organ.

Handwritten notes: Complete scale of pedals and replace pipes. Decorate front and end pipes to match. Add Pedal Principal. ~~What about~~ lower octave of Oboe, lower octave Swell Open, most keys, new knobs & labels, jambs separated (?), new lock & new keys. Decorate all old front pipes. New stool.

The 'large wood pipes ornamented' phrase is curious; the 'as built' organ utilised large metal pipes throughout on the casework, with the wooden base octave of the Pedal Open Diapason 16' remaining inside the organ. The work described as "completion scale of pedals" is the extension of the pedalboard from 25 notes (two octaves) to the current 30 notes. This work, and the completion of the lower octave of much of the Swell-work, was previously thought to have been undertaken in 1894, but the newly discovered evidence of a second phase of work in 1879 now proves that the work was carried out much earlier.

No mention is made of additional costs for all these items, and the final ledger entry relating to the works is no longer in existence: It would be reasonable to assume a considerable additional cost, and given the citation in the order for the works, it is most probable that the additional costs were borne directly by one of Aylesford's most generous benefactors, Henry Arthur Brassey, of Preston Hall.

Further, the Swell Cornopean was also extended down from Tenor C at some point, and given the lack of any evidence to the contrary, this would also appear to be the most likely time that the bottom octave was added.

For Forster & Andrews, Aylesford Parish Church organ had clearly undergone more than just a few additions and repairs: It had been physically extended with two 'wings' beyond the current inner pillars, and was now a substantial and important instrument, practically new. This is shown by their "1879" date plate in the centre of the case, in a contemporary Victorian Gothic Revival / Celtic script (as also used on their other instruments (e.g. "1886" at St Mary's, Wingham), and by other organ builders at the time (e.g. Harrison & Harrison of Durham's "1882" plate on the organ at St Mary's, Holy Island). The Aylesford plate reads "Forster & Andrews. Hull. 1879". The organ pipework was decorated, and over the next few years the casework was also decorated by a local lady (Miss Edith Login), all to match the church which itself was now decorated in the Victorian neo-Gothic style, with stencilled walls. Photographs from the period confirm this decoration. As noted from the order book, the angels were placed on the organ at this time, creating a visually impressive organ, and fairly unique.

By the end of 1879, the specification was as follows:

NOVEMBER 1879 SPECIFICATION
Forster & Andrews

Compass: Manuals CC - g3, 56 note.
Pedals CCC - F, 30 note.
Tracker Action, 3" wind.

Great
1. Open Diapason	8'	
2. Dulciana	8'	
3. Stopt Diapason	8'	
4. Principal	4'	
5. Harmonic Flute	4'	
6. Twelfth	2 ⅔'	
7. Fifteenth	2'	
8. Mixture	III	

Swell (enclosed)
9. Lieblich Bourdon	16'	
10. Open Diapason	8'	
11. Stopt. Diapason	8'	
12. Flûte d'Amour	8'	
(TC, CC-BB from No 11)		
13. Principal	4'	
14. Cornopean	8'	
15. Oboe	8'	

Pedal
16. Bourdon	16'	
17. Open Diapason	16'	
18. Principal (from No 17)	8'	

Accessories
19. Swell to Great
20. Great to Pedals
21. Swell to Pedals
22. 3 combination pedals
23. Trigger Swell pedal

(1012 pipes)

Notes:
5 renamed.
9, 10 & 15 extended CC-B (12 notes per rank).
14 extended CC-B (12 notes) (assumed).
18 new (12 pipes) Pedals extended (5 notes, C# to F).

Forster & Andrews returned to the church regularly to tune the organ, but concern was raised over the unpredictable nature of their costs, as noted in the vestry meeting minutes of 7/4/1890:

"… the Churchwardens were indebted to Messrs. Foster [*sic*] and Andrews in the sum of £20 for tuning and repairing the organ."

"Mr Brassey ... thought that it would be advisable to contract with Messrs. Foster [*sic*] and Andrews to keep the Organ in repair for a fixed sum per year.
It was resolved that the Chairman write to Messrs. Foster [*sic*] and Andrews to know their terms for keeping the organ in repair per annum".

Forster & Andrews continued to maintain the organ, although it is not clear whether this fixed-price arrangement was ever accepted.

Changes to the tonal scheme of the Forster & Andrews organ *(1894)*

The 1879 changes had made additional tonal resources available, but in moving the organ to the North Aisle Chancel it was now more remote and appeared quieter – rather than speaking into the body of the church, it now projected across the chancel, with an appreciable drop in volume as the sound travelled beyond the chancel arches into the north and south aisles. A similar effect was experienced by organists between 1965 (when the organ was moved to the main body of the church) and 2014 (after which the console was also moved), as noted in the acoustics tests below (Appendix M): Then a significant drop in the volume of the organ was experienced at the console (in the Lady Chapel).

It appears that the favoured solution in 1894 was to address the lack of a Great reed stop. Thus further works were put in hand with Forster and Andrews, in an order dated 14/4/1894. These works, completed remarkably quickly on 12/5/1894 at a cost of £55 5s, included replacing the Great Mixture with a Clarionet 8' (to Tenor C), at a cost of £19; the remainder of the costs were attributable to the site visit in April (25s), cleaning, regulating and tuning, and some re-felting.

Curiously, the Parish Magazine of May 1894 reports a somewhat lower cost:

The organ is closed for repairs, a necessary but costly process which will involve an outlay of some £30, if not more. Colonel Shaw Hellier has most kindly placed a beautiful instrument of his own, temporarily, in the Church ..."

The resulting specification can be seen, on the following page.

Forster & Andrews' maintenance was supplemented from time to time by Thomas Goodwin, who is first mentioned in the vestry minutes of 28/3/1853, in relation to the barrel organ:

> Mr Goodwin having put the organ in good repair and condition was appointed to keep it in the same state at a salary of 2£2s a year.

Five years later, the churchwarden's bill records:

> Received July 17th 1858 of the Churchwardens of Aylesford Parish the sum of Two pounds two shillings for one year tuning organ. Due Easter 1858. £2-2-0. Thomas Goodwin.

1894 SPECIFICATION
Forster & Andrews

Compass: Manuals CC - g3, 56 note.
Pedals CCC - F, 30 note.
Tracker & Pneumatic Action, 3" wind.

Great
1. Open Diapason   8'
2. Dulciana   8'
3. Stopt Diapason   8'
4. Principal   4'
5. Harmonic Flute   4'
6. Twelfth   2 2/3'
7. Fifteenth   2'
8. Clarionet (TC)   8'

Swell (enclosed)
9. Lieblich Bourdon   16'
10. Open Diapason   8'
11. Stopt. Diapason   8'
12. Flûte d'Amour   8'
    (TC, CC-BB from No 11)
13. Principal   4'
14. Cornopean   8'
15. Oboe   8'

Pedal (Flat, radiating (?))
16. Bourdon   16'
17. Open Diapason   16'
18. Principal (from No 17) 8'

Accessories
19. Swell to Great
20. Great to Pedals
21. Swell to Pedals
22. 3 combination pedals
23. Trigger Swell pedal

Notes:
8 new (replaced Mixture III, on Mixture slide).

(888 pipes)

The Maidstone Directory 1851 lists Goodwin as "Goodwin, Thomas, organ builder, Marsham street [Maidstone]", and by 1858 the Melvilles Trade Directory lists him as "Goodwin, Thomas, organ builder and pianoforte tuner, Marsham street". Goodwin continued to work on the new organ from time to time after 1865 for some years, and was paid separately (£1/19/6 early in 1895, for 'attending to the organ'); whether Forster & Andrews were ever aware of this additional work by an independent organ builder is unclear, as they tuned the organ themselves later that year (15/8/1895), at a cost of £4 (as compared with the £8/8/– for the previous year). It is possible that Goodwin may have become Forster & Andrews' local tuner and maintainer in this area, but there is no firm evidence either for or against this theory. By this latter visit, Goodwin appears to have already gone into retirement, or at least wound-up or sold his business: Whilst the Kelly's Kent Directory for Maidstone lists "Goodwin Thomas, 24 Marsham street" in 1878, there is no mention of him in the 1891 edition.

The end of an era –
The final visit of Forster & Andrews *(1908)*

Forster and Andrews were still maintaining the organ at the start of the 20th century, being called back to undertake significant work for the final time in 1908. The scope of work carried out at that time, during the incumbency of Rev Arthur Thorndike, was as follows:

> To thoroughly clean the organ, taking out all the pipes, cleaning and returning them; freeing the interior from dust, dirt & grit. Clean and lubricate all working parts (?) then regulate mechanically & musically & tune through.

In addition, the keyboards and pedalboard were re-bushed, broken reeds repaired, and some re-felting and re-leathering carried out. The cost of the 1908 works was £30.

This work may was almost certainly necessitated by the dirt and dust arising from the building works in the church (vestry extension and blocking of the old vestry doorway).

By 1910, maintenance of the organ had been entrusted to Harvey of Maidstone, and the association of Forster & Andrews with this instrument came to an end after a period of 45 years.

Harvey of Maidstone, organ builders

The Kelly's Directory of Kent, 1913 (Part 2: Private Resident & Trade Directories) lists Harvey under 'Musical Instrument Makers', 'Organ Builders', and 'Organ Tuners & Repairers' as follows: "Harvey & Co. Lower Stone street and 43 Faith street, Maidstone" *(University of Leicester Special Collections Online)*; Harvey had been listed in the 1911 edition, although in the 1909 edition, the listing is "Harvey, Lane & Co, Organ builders, Lower Stone street & 43 Faith street".

It is interesting to note that the Lower Stone Street address was also that given for William Walmsley just seven years earlier: The 1899 and 1902 editions list "Walmsley, William, organ builder. Lower Stone street", but by the 1909 edition the organ builder at this address is Harvey, not Walmsley: In the Kent Messenger Directory of Maidstone 1904 (University of Leicester Special Collections Online) we read "William Walmsley, Organ builder. Lower Stone Street / 2 Stacey's Yard". NPOR describe this as the "Lea Valley Works", although it would almost certainly have been known as the "Len Valley Works", given its location. It is likely that one of the Harvey's (father or son) took over Walmsley's business; H Harvey's father may have been apprenticed to Walmsley, as Harvey himself appears to have got into the organ building business through his father. Less clear is whether the John Walmsley (known as Jack) who was organist at Aylesford early in the last decade of the 19th century was any relation to this Walmsley, the organ builder; all that can be said with certainty is that the name was not particularly common in this part of Kent, and William Walmsley may well have been John Walmsley's Father.

By 1959, Harvey had relocated to 38 Hardy Street Maidstone, as evidenced from a letter from H Harvey to JH Thompson (Hon. Sec. to the PCC) dated 3/7/1959. Harvey was to have a long association with Aylesford, spanning 54 years, almost concurrent with the incumbency of Billy Wilson as organist. By 1964, when Harvey's responsibility for the organ ceased, the works were being carried out by H Harvey, although his father may well have been responsible for the organ in the early days of the contract.

In a footnote to the letter of 3/7/1959, Harvey provides JH Thompson (Hon. Sec. to the PCC) with the following information:

> As regards the St. Peter's Church Organ Tuning contract, that is, Four visits per year, under the original contract granted by the Rev. T.K. Sopwith, M.A. then Vicar of Aylesford in 1910. There has never been an increase in the charge I find.

I am certain that obtaining a fixed-price tuning contract for 49 years would not be a possibility today!

By the 1960s, Harvey was no longer listed in the Kelly's Trade Directories, and as he did not tender for the rebuild of Aylesford organ in 1963, it is reasonable to assume that he was by then going into retirement.

The organ at St Mark's Church, Eccles

In the letter of 3/7/1959, Harvey quotes for the maintenance of the organ at St Mark's Eccles, a mission church of the Aylesford vicar, Rev Cyril Grant, built in the 1880s and closed in 1969. The organ appears initially to have been maintained by W Walmsley of Maidstone, with significant work undertaken in 1900:

> The Organ has been removed for repairs, and the order has been given to Mr. W. Walmesley [sic], of Maidstone, for its thorough restoration. He has promised that it shall be back at Easter, and we shall have a really good instrument. (PM, March 1900)

> The original estimate has increased by the addition of some pipes to carry the principal stop through, which will be a great improvement. The organ builder hopes that he will be able to erect the organ by Easter, but some delay has occurred, for which he is not responsible, in regard to the new manuals. (PM, April 1900)

> We shall be able to use it again for the first time in Divine Service on Whit-Sunday. (PM, June 1900)

Between 1902 and 1909, Walmsley's business passed to Harvey: Although H Harvey's father worked on the Eccles organ from at least 1919 until 1921 (when Harvey himself also assisted), maintenance of the organ was in the hands of FH Browne (Canterbury), as confirmed by a letter from Thompson to FH Browne's dated 6/7/1959: "We are most grateful to you for looking after the organ all these years." We read further *(PM, August 1951)*: "In the Parish Church, and in St. Mark's, electric light has been installed. Money has been expended on the organs."

In the Parish Magazine of October 1958, Ken Wells *(using extracts from "Rambles Round Churches," Volume IV by H. Smethem [sic])* speculated on the origin of the organ in St Mark's Eccles:

In his early days the Rev. Dr. T. H. Newman, of Helmes, Hornchurch, sometime Fellow of Magdalen College, Oxford, gave an old organ to Cyril Fletcher Grant, Vicar of Aylesford, 1878-1895, for the use of the Mission Church at Eccles. Among other items in the "Inventory of goods belonging to Oliver Cromwell at Hampton Court" was: "Item: In the great hall, one large organ and a chain organ, which was brought from Maudlin College in Oxford. Value about £300 [for both organs, in 1659]." This organ, in Cyril Grant's Mission Church in Eccles, was in all probability the "chain organ of Oliver Cromwell, brought from Maudlin College." ... the one in regular use at S. Mark's Church, Eccles, today.

The source of the Eccles organ is also confirmed by Alan McCrerie. The term "chain organ" should almost certainly be "chair organ", usually referring to a small one-manual semi-mobile organ. NPOR notes that this organ had been in "a private house" before arriving in Eccles; it was exported to Australia in 1976.

Roy Lampard was organist at St Mark's Eccles for many years until the closure of the church at the end of the 1960s.

Organ blowing in Aylesford: From manual to electric blowing plant

Surprisingly little is known of the many individuals who operated the hand lever to provide the wind for the organ between 1865 and 1947, when electric blowing plant was installed. The organist would be unable to use the organ without the services of an organ blower, and thus their role was also deemed to warrant some financial remuneration. The bellows lever was installed towards the back of the organ, to the right of the console; evidence of it can still be seen in the patched panelwork. At the console, the organist would have an indication of how full the bellows were by a simple mechanism of a weight on some string on one side of the console; the weight dropped as the bellows filled. The job of organ blowing was not particularly stimulating, and evidence of boredom can be seen in the etched graffiti on the blowing panel – although many of these names were almost certainly from choir boys as well. One very clear inscription is "W STOCKFORD 1936 AGE 18", although others cover a wide period of time including one from 21/2/1886, a Sunday – clearly a long sermon that day!

Graffiti on the organ blowers panel

From 1861, we see entries in the treasurer's records for amounts paid to the organ blower. This amount varied from year to year, suggesting that the post-holder was paid on an attendance only basis; in 1861, it was £6/15/–. In the vestry meeting minutes of 12/4/1909, the payment is clearly made on a 'per occasion' basis: "It was unanimously agreed to pay Alfred Wakefield 1/6 per Sunday for this work and if the organist requires a blower at other times a person to be engaged and paid on each occasion". By 1939, the organ blower's fee is recorded as having been £3/19/–, although this may not have been for a full year.

Alfred Wakefield is one of just three organ blowers mentioned by name in official documents; 'Mitchell' is mentioned in the Parish Magazine of July 1872, and Michael Gosling, the last of the long line of organ blowers, was thanked in the June 1947 edition of the Parish Magazine:

> We take this opportunity of thanking those youths who in years now past have used their muscles to work the hand blower and we say goodbye, with gratitude, to Michael Gosling, who is the last of a long line of loyal "human blowers".

The decision to convert from hand-pumped to electric blower was taken in 1946. The PCC received a quotation for £78 10s excluding the "small building and wiring", from Roy Huntingford *(Minutes 20/5/1946)*: An outbuilding had been planned to be built against the north wall of the Chancel (Lady Chapel), to house the new blower, as per the sketch opposite:

1946: Proposed building to house mechanical organ blower at St Peter's Aylesford

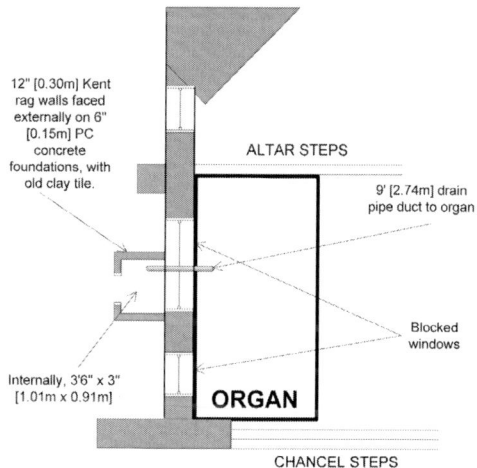

12" [0.30m] Kent rag walls faced externally on 6" [0.15m] PC concrete foundations, with old clay tile.

ALTAR STEPS

9' [2.74m] drain pipe duct to organ

Blocked windows

Internally, 3'6" x 3" [1.01m x 0.91m]

ORGAN

CHANCEL STEPS

In the event, the outbuilding was never built, the blower being installed inside the organ, against the north wall adjacent to the altar steps (as indicated by Mander's 1965 sketches of the organ), and taking air from outside through a hole in the large blocked-up window on the north side of the Chancel.

In the November 1946 edition of the Parish Magazine the writer explains that there had been difficulties with the Diocesan Advisory Committee over the installation of the blower, but were confident, having 'good hopes that the work will shortly be able to be put in hand'; by the May 1947 edition we read that,

Aylesford Church – north aisle, sometime between 1907 (as an altar appeared, which is now in the Lady Chapel) and around 1943 (when the pulpit was moved)

After many weary months of difficulty it would appear as though we may now hope to have the new blower installed within a few weeks. An application to the Chancellor of the Diocese to grant a faculty for the installation of the blower and the placing of a memorial tablet to the late Canon Everett has been applied for and we hope soon to acknowledge its receipt. The cost of the Memorial will far exceed the amount contributed and in fact will probably be upwards of £150, so we should be glad to receive additional donations.

A box to quieten the blower mechanism, as well as the trunking for the intake of the Discus blower, was constructed by Bill Linkstead, and the blower installation work was completed in 1947 by Roy Huntingford, a Gravesend engineer.

By the June 1947 edition of the Parish Magazine, it is recorded that,

At long last this [blower] has been installed and as soon as the Memorial plaque to Canon Everett is finished, arrangements will be put in hand for the unveiling and dedication service. As an illustration of the increased cost in running a church it should be noted that the original total cost of the new blower and memorial plaque was £90, but in the end the cost had risen to £150.

In the November 1947 edition of the magazine, we finally read of the memorial's installation:

MEMORIAL TABLET TO THE LATE CANON EVERETT. This really beautiful tablet of English oak, with incised and gilded lettering, with moulded frame, measuring 2ft. 11in. x 1ft. 11in., was dedicated on October 19th, at 11 a.m., by the Venerable the Archdeacon of Rochester, who also preached the sermon.

The oak memorial was mounted on the north wall of the church, to the east of the organ (and moved onto the east side of the organ case in 2012, when cupboards were built along the north wall). The text reads:

FREDERICK JOHN EVERETT
HONORARY CANON AND RURAL DEAN
was from 1915 to 1941 the faithful
VICAR OF AYLESFORD
The parishioners and others by whom he was
so greatly loved have installed in this Church a
mechanical organ blower to commemorate
his devoted ministration in the service of God
1946

Early modernisation and tonal enhancements to the organ *(1947)*

Other than general maintenance and tuning, carried out by Harvey, little work was done on the organ until after the Second World War. The first serious threat to the organ came in the middle of the war when an external "Report on the fabric of the church" was produced, dated 20/5/1943. It was commented of the "North Chapel" in section J, that "This would be much improved by the removal of the organ to a different place or by its replacement by an instrument requiring less room." An undated Church Guide by Rev R W Walls (Curate at Aylesford in the mid-1940s) seized on this point: "The organ stands in the north chancel. While being a good instrument, it prevents the chancel being properly and neatly furnished as a chapel." The recommended move of the organ was not quoted for in the 1943 report, and more than 20 years were to elapse until it was finally executed.

Some works were undertaken in the near term, however: After the blower was installed early in 1947, further works on the organ were undertaken by Harvey that year, at a cost of around £120. No documentary evidence has been found to confirm the scope of the works, but a conversation in 1987 with Tom Tomkin, a churchwarden at the time of the rebuild, provided details, which (with the exception of the balanced Swell pedal) can be confirmed from the notes made by Mander's when surveying the organ in 1963. A Trumpet stop was added to the Great, obtained from a Wren church in London destroyed by enemy action: It cost £20 to purchase and was paid for equally by Harold Moore, the then new organist, and Tom W Tomkin. Two foot couplers were added (for Swell to Great and Great to Pedal), termed 'ankle tappers' by Harold Moore, and the trigger Swell pedal was replaced by a balanced Swell pedal.

Very limited information exists on how this work was funded: Whilst the Trumpet was purchased as indicated above, there was also an organ fund (into which ex-chorister Mr Joy donated an £8 cheque, as recorded by the note of thanks in the Parish Magazine November 1947), although this fund had historically also been used to pay for the organist and organ blowers.

The resultant specification can be seen overleaf.

As the organ approached its 100th anniversary, significant work became necessary.

Before considering this though, it is worth reviewing those who have played the organ at Aylesford, and looking at the choir, whose singing has been accompanied by it for a century and a half.

1947 SPECIFICATION
Harvey

Compass:	Manuals CC - g3, 56 note.
	Pedals CCC - F, 30 note.
	Tracker & Pneumatic Action, 3" wind.

Great

1. Open Diapason — 8'
2. Dulciana — 8'
3. Stopt Diapason — 8'
4. Principal — 4'
5. Harmonic Flute — 4'
6. Twelfth — 2 ⅔'
7. Fifteenth — 2'
8. Trumpet — 8'
9. Clarionet (TC) — 8'

Pedal

17. Bourdon — 16'
18. Open Diapason — 16'
19. Principal (from No 18) — 8'

Swell (enclosed)

10. Lieblich Bourdon — 16'
11. Open Diapason — 8'
12. Stopt. Diapason — 8'
13. Flûte d'Amour — 8'
    (TC, CC-BB from No 12)
14. Principal — 4'
15. Cornopean — 8'
16. Oboe — 8'

Accessories

20. Swell to Great
21. Great to Pedals
22. Swell to Pedals
23. 3 combination pedals
24. Balanced Swell pedal

(944 pipes)

Notes:
8 – New: 2nd hand pipework on Clarionet slide.
9 – Moved from main soundboard to off-note chest.
20 & 21 duplicated on foot pistons.
24 New: replaced Trigger Swell pedal.
New electric blower.

Organists and assistant organists

The nineteenth century organists

Even though the barrel organ was largely automatic, it required a person (usually known as a 'grinder') to turn the handle, select the desired tune, and draw the required stops; they did not need to be skilled in music. In the vestry meeting minutes of 25/3/1837, we read, "It was Resolv'd on the proposal of the vicar that Mr John Wagon be appointed to take charge of the organ, to be erected in the church, and to perform the respective services at a salary of five pounds ... arising & to be paid from the rents of the Church Lands." Entries in the treasurer's books for 1842 and 1844 confirm this salary *(21/6/1842, 11/11/1842 & 15/11/1844)*.

John Wagon was also "Keeper of accounts and collector of Rates for the Parish" *(vestry minutes 25/3/1846)*, "Collector of Rates and Keeper of the Parish accounts with a yearly salary of Twenty pounds, payable out of the Poor Rate" *(vestry minutes 25/3/1848)* and "Surveyor with a salary of sixteen pounds per year" *(vestry minutes 25/3/1848 and thereafter until at least 26/3/1855)*.

The barrel organ was installed in 1838. John Wagon remained as organist until 1864, shortly before the new Forster and Andrews instrument was built in 1865. In the vestry meeting minutes of 28/3/1864, it is recorded that, "J Wagon having resigned the office of Organist (after 27 years service) Mr Silas Wagon was thereupon appointed in his stead."

The January 1866 edition of the Parish Magazine records that:

> A meeting was held at the Vicarage on Monday, Dec 18th, to determine the steps to be taken to provide an Organist for the Church. A committee, consisting of the Vicar, Churchwardens, and Messrs. Keddell, Woolley, and Hammond, were appointed to engage an organist, and it was agreed that the salary should be raised by subscription. About £10 was promised in the room, and an appeal will be made to all Pew Holders to make up the required sum – about £30. This we have no doubt will be easily raised. Subscriptions will be received by Rev S W Phillips, and Messrs. Shaw and Cole.

Ken Wells (letters 17/1/1988) believes that the Woolley mentioned as being a member of the committee was the father of Harold Woolley (who later became organist): This is likely, as Harold Woolley's father, Henry Lowe Woolley, was active in the church at this

time, his death occurring in 1887 *(PM, April 1887)*. The Maidstone Telegraph of 8/12/1860 records Keddell as "assistant-surgeon". It is interesting to note that this selection meeting was held just over a week after the organ's opening service of Friday 8/12/1865, and that the sole purpose of the gathering appears to have been to appoint an organist; although no documentary evidence exists, it is quite possible that Silas Wagon decided, having been appointed only the previous year, that the new organ was beyond his capabilities, and that a trained organist was required.

The following month, under "Church and School Notes", we read:

> Mr John Humphreys, late Queen's scholar of St Mark's Training College, and bearing a Government Certificate, has been appointed Organist in the Parish Church, with a salary of £25 per annum.

John Humphreys also became master of the school in Bull Lane, and, later that year, master of the national school, in succession to John Wagon.

Harold Woolley, a pupil of John Hopkins (see below) succeeded John Humphreys as organist at the end of 1879, with a recorded salary of £57/4/– in 1880. It is unclear why John Humphreys resigned his organist post, although it may have been due to retirement. Harold Woolley gave a number of recitals, including those on 26/7/1882 and 28/8/1882 *(PM, August 1882)*. In 1883, the organist's salary was recorded as being £45 per annum. In the September 1952 edition of the Parish Magazine, Billy Wilson continued his "Aylesford Fifty Years Ago" series with an article on "Parish Organists": Wilson met Woolley when the former was organist and the latter an old man:

> From all accounts he was a wonderful organist. In fact, he was regarded as a genius. A pupil of Dr Hopkins, of Rochester Cathedral ... he had for a fellow pupil a young man who was knighted for his distinguished musical career, Sir Frederick Bridge.

Dr John Hopkins (1822-1900) was the younger brother of Dr Edward John Hopkins (1818-1901), organist at Temple Church London between 1843 and 1898, and writer of a number of chants and hymn tunes (including "Ellers" ("Saviour, again to thy dear name") and "St Hugh" ("Lord, teach us how to pray aright")). John Hopkins was organist at Rochester Cathedral from 1856 until 1900; Edward Hopkins' first cousin, John Larkin Hopkins (1819-1873) preceded John Hopkins as organist of Rochester Cathedral, between 1841 and 1856.

In the February 1986 edition of the Parish Magazine, Ken Wells provided some reminiscences on Woolley, including an interesting anecdote, editorially entitled "An Organist of Spirit":

> Mr Brassey, of Preston Hall, offered to pay Woolley's fees to the Royal Academy of Music, but Woolley declined, claiming, probably correctly, that the academy could teach him nothing about music that he did not already know. All it could give him would be a certificate ... It is said that on numerous occasions he had to be led straight from the public house to the church when he was due to play the organ for the evening service. Indeed, many people declared that he could play the organ even better when drunk than he could sober.

Further evidence of Woolley's abilities are found in the Kent Messenger and Maidstone Telegraph of 27/5/1882:

> Choral Service at Aylesford. On Sunday evening last [i.e. 21/5/1882] a special choral service ... was held in the Parish Church, which was crowded to standing room, many remaining outside to hear the service. The artistic skill and taste displayed by the organist, Mr.H.Wooley, needs no further comment than to say that the playing was masterly throughout, while an efficient orchestra supplemented the performance on the organ.

Ken Wells *(letters 23/1/1988, and PM February 1986)* continues:

> People came from miles around just to hear him play ... He played the giant organ at the Crystal Palace and was given a standing ovation.

The relationships influencing music at Aylesford during this period are worth further detailed exploration.

Whilst the appointment of John Humphreys may well have been influenced by the cathedral, where the vicar (Rev Anthony Grant) was also a canon, it is almost certain that Harold Woolley, as a pupil of the cathedral organist would have been an obvious successor to John Humphreys, early in the incumbency of Rev Anthony Grant's son, Cyril.

Harold Woolley, an Aylesford local, had been organist at King Street Church Maidstone (a Baptist church, opened 28/5/1861, on a site now occupied by an estate agents

premises and part of the Chequers shopping centre): The organ from that church was built by Thomas Goodwin in 1867, with a specification similar to the Forster & Andrews at Aylesford; it was moved to St Martin of Tours Church Detling by Colin Savage and Ron Parratt in 1973, and was rebuilt by FH Browne in 1995. Given the association with the Baptist church, the "Organist of Spirit" comment probably requires some tempering, as that church would have been strictly against drinking.

Harold Woolley had played a concert at Aylesford Infants schoolroom on 24/10/1870, attended (amongst others) by the Brasseys *(Maidstone Telegraph, 29/10/1870)*, who had barely been in Preston Hall a month. HA Brassey appeared to have treated Woolley, a pupil of John Hopkins, the cathedral organist, as something of a protégé: Although Woolley appeared to spurn the certification of his skills, he is cited on the order for the initial works on the organ in February 1879, and described as "Prof. Music", whilst John Humphreys was still the incumbent organist: Woolley was associated with the organ at Aylesford even before he became the Parish organist, and the "Prof. Music" title may have been Brassey's complimentary description of him, to ensure that Forster & Andrews took heed of his advice. The scope of the November 1879 works – extended as indicated by the handwritten notes on the order book – are highly likely to have been influenced by Harold Woolley, being given a 'free hand' by the vicar, and the funding by HA Brassey (whose main influence is most likely to have been the decorative scheme and the angels). Harold Woolley became organist of Aylesford church immediately after the rebuild and expansion of the organ in November 1879, and thus it can be surmised that Brassey used the rebuild as a 'hook' to engineer his local, and very competent, protégé into the vacant organist's position, on the recommendation of the cathedral organist with the support of the vicar.

The diagram in Appendix I attempts to clarify this complex relationship between key people in both Rochester Cathedral and Aylesford, and the most likely influences and activities.

Harold Woolley remained organist until Jack Walmsley's appointment in 1890; the organist's salary dropped to £35 per annum, and in 1894/5 it was £30; the treasurer's records show £35 for 1894, with £30 pencilled in alongside. Billy Wilson wrote, in September 1952:

> Following Mr Woolley was Mr Walmsley, who … was another splendid organist and choirmaster. As a boy, he was solo-chorister at St George's Chapel, Windsor … He

came to Aylesford in the dual capacity of Organist and Assistant Master in the Boy's School ... Later we [Jack Walmsley and Billy Wilson] were colleagues together as Assistant Masters in the school, under that excellent Headmaster, Mr Dine.

We also read that H Burgiss-Brown played for the Brassey Memorial dedication service in 1892 *(Sussex Agricultural Express, 29/10/1892)*, although his playing seems at most to have been on an occasional basis only. Eric Dine performed the role of assistant organist on occasion, up to the arrival of Rev and Mrs Thorndike, in 1902; the Kent Messenger 1904 Directory of Maidstone records Eric Dine as "Master at the Boys' School", and John [Jack] Walmsley as "Assistant Overseer" (and "Clerk of the Parish Council").

John (Jack) Walmsley (organist 1890-c.1895, & c.1916-1919)

Jack Walmsley also ran a Choral Society, which "under Mr Walmesley's [sic] efficient direction, has greatly prospered ..." *(PM, December 1893).*

Around 1895, Charles Manglesdorff, ARCO, ARCM, was appointed organist, being paid a salary of £6/5/– in 1896, and £7/10/– by 1900: Charles Manglesdorff is listed as "The Organist and Choirmaster" on the massive and artistic "Aylesford Almanack 1897" *(which can be viewed in Kent Library & Archive Centre, ref. P12/28/55).*

Jack Walmsley had resigned the organist's position "because of his religious principles" *(PM, July 1970)*: Aylesford Church was increasingly following the tenets of the Oxford Movement, and this was to come to a head in 1900. Jack Walmsley appears to have continued to be active in the church, as a Sidesperson and as an attendee at most vestry meetings right up until 1915. At the end of the First World War, he covered for Billy Wilson as organist and choir master, whilst the latter was at war (as noted below).

1900: A year of turmoil

As indicated above ("Aylesford Church restorations in the Victorian era"), the influence of the Oxford Movement was felt at least to some extent in Aylesford, evidenced most visibly in the church decorative scheme undertaken in 1879. The liturgy of the church, with an organist and a competent (and now robed) choir, would lend itself well to the greater 'sobriety in worship'; the appointment and institution of Rev George Vaux at the end of 1895 *(PMs, November and December 1895)* was to bring the liturgical reform to

a head in a debacle entitled "No popery" by Billy Wilson, in his recounting of the events following Vaux's appointment *(PM, July 1952)*:

> Unfortunately, as the months went on, certain innovations were introduced into the Church by the new Vicar [Rev George Vaux] which did not meet with the approval of a large section of the parishioners, who showed their disapproval in no uncertain manner. Strong objections were taken to the wearing of Vestments at Holy Communion and to other devotional practices at the same service. Charges were brought against the Vicar of trying to introduce Roman Catholicism into the Church. Great resentment was felt when the Processional Cross made its appearance, and when it was put to use at the head of processions, the congregation, with the exception of a few members, left their seats and filed out of the church. The senior members of the choir refused to follow the Cross in the procession from the Chancel round the Church, and back to the Chancel. Instead they remained in the Choir Stalls whilst the Cross bearer, Choir Boys and Clergy proceeded round the Church singing a hymn. The usual hymn was "Onward Christian Soldiers," and the procession started at the beginning of the third verse, "At the sign of triumph, Satan's host doth flee." The people left their pews and crowded out in front of the choir, bringing the procession to a standstill.

> One suspects that these words for the commencement of the procession rather suited the Vicar. Open-air protest meetings were held on the Bank, the assistance of the Kensitites was obtained [John Kensit (1853-1902) was an anti-ritualist and founder of the Protestant Trust Society, which opposed the excessive influence of the Oxford Movement on the Church of England], but all efforts of the parishioners to make the Vicar change his principles were unsuccessful. Many of the congregation forsook the Church and went over to the Wesleyan Church [later Aylesford Methodist Church, now closed], but others, although objecting to the ritual, remained faithful to their Parish Church. Altogether it was a sad state of affairs, and its effect was felt and remembered for many years. In 1902 the Rev. G. B. Vaux went to Carshalton. He died a year or two ago [i.e. late 1940s] in Oxfordshire, at the age of 91.

"Dissatisfaction" with the vicar is noted in the Parish Magazines of 1899, on such issues as "service times"; the vestry meeting minutes of 16/4/1900 provide interesting reading:

> Present: Rev G B Vaux (Chairman), John Walmsley, Silas Wagon, Wm Leegood and Geo. L Hawkes [and others]:

Mr Walmsley said that the Parishioners had complained at the way in which the services had been conducted by the Vicar and he wished it to be recorded on the minutes that the Inhabitants objected to his teaching and he hoped the Vicar would have a meeting of the Inhabitants to discuss the various matters in connection with the Church service. He complained of wafer bread being used at Communion and said he could not partake of the Sacrament because he was not in love and charity with the Vicar.

Mr G L Hawkes objected to the Altar Book being used by the children.

Mr Leegood objected to the use of candles on the Altar.

After others had spoken the Vicar said with reference to the Altar Book of which complaint had been made to the Lord Bishop of Rochester, the Bishop had returned the copy with the remark that he entirely agreed with the information contained therein and he thought it a most useful book.

With reference to the bread used at Holy Communion he said wafer bread had never been used by him and he did not intend using it.

Mr Walmsley apologised and the meeting ended.

Reconciliation of sorts had clearly occurred between vicar and congregation by the time Rev Vaux moved on from Aylesford: In the vestry meeting minutes of 31/3/1902, Rev G B Vaux "thanked the vestry for their expressions of good feeling & said he should never forget the great kindness he had received during the time he had been Vicar of the Parish".

Charles Manglesdorff continued as organist and choirmaster until 1902, when a new era was ushered in by the appointment of Rev Arthur Thorndike, a canon at Rochester Cathedral (and father of the actress Sybil Thorndike and actor Russell Thorndike) as vicar.

Organists and assistant organists since the early twentieth century

When Rev A J W Thorndike became vicar in 1902, he also took over the duties of choirmaster. Mrs Thorndike, "a fine pianist and organist" (Ken Wells, PM September 1987) became organist. In the vestry meeting minutes of 1/4/1907, we note that it was resolved "That a vote of thanks be given to Mrs Thorndike for her kindness in returning

the sum of £12.10.– from her salary as Organist, towards Church Expenses", and again, from the meeting of 20/4/1908 that "... a vote of thanks be given to Mrs Thorndike for her service during the past year, and for her kindness in returning to the churchwardens the sum of £7 out of her salary as organist besides paying for the music and other expenses in connection with the choir".

The Thorndikes left Aylesford in 1909, whereupon Billy Wilson was appointed organist, as belatedly recorded in the vestry meeting minutes of 28/3/1910, with the vicar (Rev Thos. Karl Sopwith) as Chairman, and amongst those present, Silas Wagon (briefly organist in the mid 1860s)):

> The Chairman stated that since Mrs Thorndike left the Parish, William E Wilson had been engaged as Organist at a salary at the rate of £20 per year. He was very pleased with the improvement he had made since he undertook the duties, and he thought he was entitled to an increased salary.

William E (Billy) Wilson
(Organist 1909-1946)

> Mr C M Wood proposed that Wilson receive in future £25 per year. This was seconded by Mr Geo. L Hawkes and carried unanimously.

The Kent Messenger 1904 Directory of Maidstone records William Wilson as "Parish Clerk" (and also "Newsagent", although Parish Magazines advertise the "Newsagent and tobacconist" as "V E Wilson").

Billy Wilson served for some time in the First World War, alongside many members of the choir (as noted below). The Parish Magazine of June 1919 welcomed home the soldiers from the war, including:

> Mr W E Wilson, who has resumed charge of the choir ... We gladly take this opportunity of expressing our indebtedness to Mr Walmesley [sic] and to the boys who stayed at home for the way they have carried on during a time of great difficulty.

Billy Wilson's Presentation "to mark his 37 years as Organist at the Parish Church" was approved by the PCC in their meeting of 22/1/1947, and in their meeting of 17/6/1946 referred to "the brilliant playing of Mr W E Wilson", and to the "very high qualities of

Mr W E Wilson as an Organist & Choirmaster". With some 37 years' service (as well as assisting for some years after he resigned), Billy Wilson is currently the longest serving organist; however, little is recorded of his incumbency. We do discover that, in 1939, he was paid £30 for his services. Further, those who served under him in the choir (including Ken Wells) remembered him with deep respect. He remained active in the church even after he stopped playing, being regularly recorded in the Parish Magazine as a sidesman until January 1959; he is mentioned again in the November 1961 edition of the Parish Magazine as being "over 70 years in one place."

During most of Billy Wilson's time as organist, the vicar was Rev Frederick Everett (vicar from 1915 until his death in 1941); Mrs Everett filled the role of assistant organist during this time: Ken Wells *(letters, 2/2/1988)* states that

> She often played for our Sunday School Services on Sunday afternoons, 1920s onwards, and whenever Billy Wilson was not available. Also for special Sunday Afternoon Services such as those held for 'Toc H' and other organisations who held special services from time to time.

Billy Wilson was to remain organist and choirmaster until his resignation "at the end of June [1946]" *(Annual Church Meeting Minutes, 24/4/1946)*. In the June 1947 edition of the Parish Magazine, the vicar (Rev H T Southgate) noted that Billy Wilson had wished to resign before, but undertook initially to remain whilst Canon Everett was alive, and then again for a short while into Harry Southgate's incumbency:

> ... he consented to serve until the war was over and there was some chance of obtaining the services of a suitable successor.

Harold F Moore (FIGCM – Fellow of the Incorporated Guild of Church Musicians) was appointed organist from June 1946, as recorded in the Parish Magazine of July 1948:

> Mr H F Moore of Snodland ... comes to us with a fine record of long and splendid service to the church at Sutton Valence.

Billy Wilson continued to stand-in for Harold Moore during 1947, and again into the 1950s, when Harold Moore was away or off sick (for example, the Hymn Singing Service on 3/8/1952). In the January 1948 edition of the Parish Magazine, we read:

THANKS are herewith conveyed to all those in the augmented choir who gave such pleasure to so many at the Musical Service on November 27th. Both the choir work and the solos and duets were very finely rendered and much appreciated. Owing to his accident Mr. Moore was unable to be at the organ and the sympathy and good wishes of all went out to him as he lay at home in bed with a cut head, bruises and a broken arm. Great must have been his disappointment at being absent, but he knew his choir would carry on successfully and they

Harold Moore (organist 1946-1969), at the old console (pre-1965)

certainly did. A great many words would be necessary adequately to describe the gratitude we all felt to Mr. Wilson, who at a moment's notice took Mr. Moore's place at the organ to accompany music, the practice of which he had had nothing to do with. Many experts would have refused at such short notice, but not our Mr. Wilson. He felt he must get us out of the difficulty which Mr. Moore's accident had placed us in. In spite of his own diffidence, we know his fine capabilities and of course everything went off beautifully. Thank you, Mr. Wilson; and thank you, choir and soloists; and thanks also to Mr. Moore, whose marvellous escape from death we rejoice over.

In 1947, Harold Moore was responsible for initiating works by Harvey on the organ (as outlined above). In 1965, towards the end of his incumbency, he was also responsible for the major work of moving, rebuilding, extending and electrifying the organ, commemorated by a brass plaque on the organ case. The scope of the 1965 work is detailed below.

Harold Moore is mentioned in the Parish Magazine of March 1951:

HONOUR FOR AYLESFORD ORGANIST
We have pleasure in making it known that our organist, Mr. H. F. Moore, has been made by examination a Fellow of the Incorporated Guild of Church Musicians. A high standard of musical knowledge and execution is requisite for such a distinction to be bestowed. It may have passed unnoticed that from time to time we sing music in church composed by Mr. Moore. The Te Deum and Benedicite in particular are instances of his ability. We are sure that members of the choir and congregation and his many friends will join in congratulation.

As well as being a fine organist and choirmaster, Harold Moore also possessed a dry sense of humour: An amusing statement appears in the September 1961 edition of the Parish Magazine:

> The Church organist, Mr. Harold Moore, is grateful for the ham sandwich left on the organ seat by a visitor to Aylesford Church.

On 12/11/1969, the PCC recorded receiving a letter of resignation from Harold Moore, owing to ill health; whilst he continued to play occasionally in early 1970, he died on 28/11/1970: Les Jackson paid tribute to him *(PM, January 1971)* as follows:

> [Harold] had a gravel voice and a case hardened exterior, but ... [he] had a heart of gold and a charitable disposition to match.

The memorial plaque to Harold Moore, and to the move of the organ in 1965, was approved by the PCC on 16/3/1971; the text of the plaque is reproduced below, in the description of the 1965 work.

The March 1970 Parish Magazine records the appointment of Peter Dawson (LRAM, LLCM), then aged 24, to succeed Harold Moore. Peter Dawson moved away from Aylesford, resigning his position as organist and choirmaster from the end of December 1974; he was succeeded in February 1975 by Roy Burgess (LRAM).

Peter Dawson
(organist 1969-1974)

Roy Burgess
(organist 1975-1985)

Ten years later, the PCC meeting of 3/7/1985 noted a letter from Roy Burgess, resigning his position from 1st September 1985; the organist post was advertised, and a small selection committee set-up, comprising the vicar (Rev Arthur Heathcote) and a few members of the PCC and choir.

The current organist, and author of this historical guide, took-up duties in September 1985 (then aged 25): The first service at Aylesford was the Harvest Festival, on Sunday afternoon, 29/9/1985.

The Forster & Andrews organ case, Aylesford Church, 2008

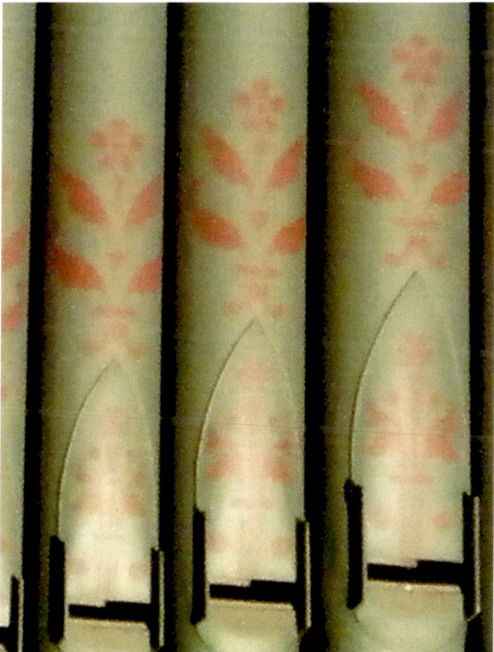

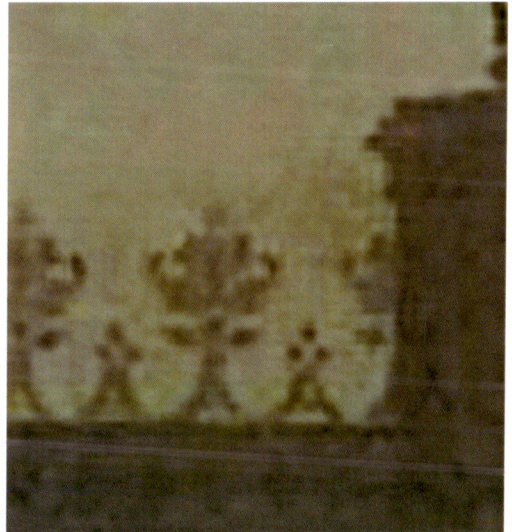

Detailed pictures showing the decoration of the church walls in the late nineteenth century, with the matching stencilled (largely hidden) organ case pipework

338.

Aylesford Church

1865	Great cc		Swell cc	
1 Dec	1 Open	56	1 Lieb. Bordun	44
	2 Dulciana	56	2. Op (prep to cc)	44
	3 Stopt Diap.	56	3. Stopt	56
	4 Principal	56	4. Fl. d' Am (to 3)	44
	5 Fl. Trav. 4'	56	5 Principal	56
	6 Twelfth	56	6. Cornop (prep to cc)	44
	7 Fifteenth	56	7. Oboe	44
	8 Mixture	168		308
		560	Couplers	
	Pedal		1 Swell to Great	
	1. Bourdon	25	2 Great to Pedals	

Three Composition Pedals.

1865 . 12 Dec Rec. £271. 1. 0   £ 270 " "
Carriage

Com. to Mr J. Hopkins. Rochester £20

Aylesford organ – original Forster & Andrews ledger book, 1865

Repairs & Additions

Marsh Street, Walthamstow
No. 547.

30 Notes radiating & concave Pedals - New Rollers &d.
alterations to stickers & trackers - Extension of roller frame
New &d &d. for extra pipes to .... - Machinery &c | 27 | 5 | .
Cleaning & regulating .... | 10 | . | .
Attaching Ped. Stops to Composition Pedals | 3 | . | .
Releathering Pedal Pallets | 2 | . | .

| | 42 | 5 | . |
Reduction by doing all at same time | 2 | 5 | . |
£ | 40 | . | . |

a/c

April 1879

Chas. A. Bartholomew.

Aylesford Church
No. 375

Pedal Open Diapason | 70 | . | .
Swell to Pedals Coupler | 10 | . | .
New Bellows | 15 | . | .

Complete

Feb. 1879

o/c

Rev. Cyril Grant . Aylesford. Kent
H. A. Brassey . M.P. Preston Hall . Aylesford
J. C. Woolley. Prof. Music.

Aylesford organ – original Forster & Andrews ledger book, February 1879

Repairs & Additions

Ronchurch Church

Remove [...] Bellows Feeders — 24 . .
Cleaning [...] pipes . . — 1 . .

£ 25 . .

Rev. Dr. Maddock . . . . a/c

Aylesford Church
No. 375

Ordered by H. A. Brassey. M.P. 4th June. 1879

Alter the form of Organ and place it against the
North Wall of Aisle, shewing large wood
pipes ornamented at end [...],
making Instrument wider as shewn in
tracing, with figures of [...] top of posts

Without figures — 87 . .
[...] figures — 30 . .
[...] Sir J. Brander — 14 . .

All the improvements would be enclosed and
have the appearance of being a portion of the
original Organ. — [...]
[...]
Add [...] Principal — [...]
[...]
[...]
[...]

Aylesford organ – original Forster & Andrews ledger book, November 1879

Aylesford angels (1879), following restoration, October 2014

Manufacturer nameplate on organ case (1879 rebuild)

RESTORED BY
F.H.BROWNE & SONS
ORGAN BUILDERS
CANTERBURY
2015

Organ builder nameplate on
organ case (2015 restoration)

In memory of HAROLD MOORE
ORGANIST AND CHOIRMASTER 1946-1969
under whose direction this organ was
restored and moved from the chancel.

Plaque in memory of Harold Moore, on organ case

The above photograph shows the temporary position of the organ at the east end of the North Aisle Chapel (now the Lady Chapel), thus prior to move against chancel arch & pulpit in November 1879, but after dismantling of gallery in 1878, i.e. between February and late 1879

Detailed enlargement of the photograph above, showing the organ in its temporary position

Detail of the organ pipes

Detail of the organ case panelling, painted by
Miss Edith Login (completed 1907), 2008

The organ as a
backdrop for
Lenny Bunn's
"It's Your Time"
pop video 2014

Aylesford Choir, 1989

Aylesford Choir, 2004

Aylesford Choir, 2013

ROBIN TURNER

The vital role of assistant organists has always been recognised, generally including the accompaniment of choir anthems whist the organist / choirmaster conducted the choir. The first record of an assistant (i.e. not the regular organist) is from 1892, when the Sussex Agricultural Express notes that during the service to unveil and dedicate the new Brassey Memorial window, the organ was "played by Mr. H. Burgiss-Brown" (29/10/1892). This practice was formalised in the late 1960s: In the January 1968 edition of the Parish Magazine, the vicar (Rev Alec T Goodrich) wrote:

> I have appointed Helen Turner of Larkfield as deputy-organist of our Parish Church. She ... has played the organ for school services at Aylesford during the last eighteen months.

Michael Keays (organist 1985-) & Helen Turner (assistant organist 1968-) at the Mander console, 2010-11

After 47 years, Mrs Turner is still the very able holder of this position today. The musical partnership of Michael Keays and Helen Turner has now lasted 30 years.

Until 2000, other organists also played on an occasional basis, including Dr John Brown, Alan McCrerie (formerly organist at Aylesford Methodist Church), and Christopher Haydon (the son of the Curate Rev Christine Haydon); it is hoped that the restoration of the organ in 2015 will encourage others to consider using the organ to offer their services on at least an occasional basis.

A comprehensive list of organists and assistant organists is provided in Appendix F.

The choir and music of the parish

The formation of a choir

The first mention of Aylesford church choir is in the Maidstone and Kentish Journal *(18/12/1865)*, where a report of a tea party in the Boys' National Schoolroom notes that the address was "interspersed by carols rendered by the church choir." This was just a few days after the opening of the new organ, at which the choir had been provided by the cathedral. The genesis of Aylesford church choir really dates from early 1866, when John Humphreys (organist 1866-1880) developed an unrobed, all male, choir: This new choir were doubtless encouraged by the singing of the cathedral choir and rapidly grew in confidence and ability. We learn from the Parish Magazine of May 1866 that on Easter Day 1866 (1/4/1866), the Psalms were chanted by the choir for the evening service for the first time "... and as the experiment seems to have given much satisfaction, it will be repeated on the evenings of Ascension Day and Whitsun-Day ...". Evening services had only begun in Aylesford Church on 17/1/1864, when paraffin lamps had been installed "at a cost of between £40 and £50" *(Dover Express, 23/1/1864)*. By the end of 1866, Psalms were being chanted on the last Sunday of every month (PM, November 1866), and by the following Easter (21/4/1867), "a full choral service was held [in the evening], for the first time" *(PM, May 1867)*.

In October 1866, the choir consisted of 16 voices (8 trebles, 3 altos, 3 tenors, 2 basses); this had increased by May 1867 to 18 voices (9 trebles, 3 altos, 2 tenors, 4 basses), when the choir visited Rochester Cathedral for a Choral Festival. Reports on further participation in these annual Festivals at Rochester provide details of how the choir was expanding:
- 21 voices (12 trebles, 3 altos, 3 tenors, 3 basses) on 28/5/1868 *(PM, June 1868)*
- 25 voices (15 trebles, 4 altos, 3 tenors, 3 basses) on 27/5/1869 *(PM, June 1869)*
- 27 voices (16 trebles, 4 altos, 3 tenors, 4 basses) on 19/5/1870 *(PM, June 1870)*

However, for the festival on 6/6/1872, just 14 choristers were present from Aylesford *(PM, July 1872)*.

A report in the Maidstone Telegraph, of 21/3/1868, describes a concert in Aylesford, concluding with a statement of the "efficiency of the choir, of which ... many of the larger villages might be proud." Further, the report in the Kent Messenger and Maidstone Telegraph, of 27/5/1882 (partly quoted above) states:

> Choral Service at Aylesford. On Sunday evening last a special choral service, in aid of the Choir Funds, was held in the Parish Church … The choir sang with great taste and judgement and it would be difficult to find a village choir to surpass it in the County.

The choir was recorded as "unsurpliced" for the 1870 Rochester Choral Festival *(PM, June 1870),* and were even described as "the best unsurpliced choir of all" in the Rochester Festival of 12/6/1873 *(PM, June 1873)*, where the choir "… occupied its usual place in the front row …". The move to the new choir stalls in the Church Chancel took place in 1879, and it is most likely that this is the point at which the choir began to robe.

In the Treasurer's Records of 1893, surplices were purchased at a cost of £1/10/–: Each year thereafter almost £2 was spent on washing the surplices, a practice which had stopped by the 1930s when "our mums would wash our surplices. (unpaid)." *(Ken Wells, letters, 17/1/1988)*. In 1898, the choir "appeared in new cassocks and surplices on Easter Day …" *(PM, May 1898)*, part of a gradual move towards greater dignity within the services, encouraged by Rev Vaux (as noted above). Six new surplices, at a cost of 2s 6d each, were required in 1907 *(PM July 1907)*. In the early 20th century, the choir-boys were attired in stiff white linen collars and "mortar-boards" when they attended church on a Sunday. Further, Billy Wilson, stated, "I have been asked if I remember the time when the choir did not robe. My answer is no. They wore cassocks and surplices during and before my time." *(Billy Wilson, in "Aylesford Fifty Years Ago", PM, September 1952).* Choir robes were in need of replenishment by the 1950s, with Harold Moore appealing for between £80 and £100 *(PM, September 1950)*; the PCC approved the "purchase of three more robes" in their meeting of 6/2/1952. More choir robes were purchased at a cost of £800 in 1980, as the choir expanded further *(PCC Minutes, 24/3/1980)*.

We find the first reference to choir pay in the treasurer's records of 1890, with an amount of £3/1/6 being paid to the choir boys. This was increased to £4/5/6 in 1891.

Information provided by Ken Wells *(letters 17/1/1988)* indicated that choirboys' pay in the 1930s was 1d for each attendance (one practice night per week, plus Matins & Evensong on Sundays), and 6d for each 8am communion service (Easter Day and other festivals). Full service and practice attendance would earn 12/6 per year. Weddings, funerals and other special functions were paid at the rate of 6d each. Treasurer's records indicate that choir boys' pay totalled £9/15/6 for 1939.

The history of the choir from the mid-1890s was recorded by Billy Wilson, as part of the "Aylesford Fifty Years Ago" series in the Parish Magazine. In the July 1952 edition, we read:

> In 1896 [actually late 1895] the Rev. G. B. Vaux became Vicar, and the following year, 1897, was the wonderful year of the Diamond Jubilee of Queen Victoria, commemorated in grand style all over the country. Services of thanksgiving were held in all places of worship, and the Parish Church Choir took part in such a service at All Saints', Maidstone, the only time I remember Aylesford Choir being invited to participate in a service in the County Town.

The choir in the early twentieth century

The early history of the choir is continued in Billy Wilson's "Aylesford Fifty Years Ago" article from the August 1952 edition of the Parish Magazine:

> In 1902, after the departure of the Rev. G. B. Vaux, came the Rev. A. J. W. Thorndike, from St. Margaret's, Rochester. Being possessed with a lovely baritone voice, he quickly took on the role of choirmaster, and Mrs. Thorndike, being an accomplished organist, took on those duties. Aylesford has for many years had a splendid choir. Previous to 1900, when Mr. Walmsley was organist, the choir was a good one, and Mr. Mandlesdorff continued to maintain the excellent singing. Owing to the latter living in Maidstone, one practice a week was the order of the day. When the new Vicar and Mrs. Thorndike undertook the musical duties they spared no effort to continue the tradition and even to make improvements. They both enjoyed this sphere of work and their enthusiasm spread to the choir.
>
> Almost every evening the choir boys went to the Vicarage for practice with Mrs. Thorndike to do voice training and to prepare for the following Sunday services, or to practice music for special occasions. Then followed indoor games or games in the Vicarage meadow. The full practice on a Thursday evening was an education in the art of rendering church music, strict attention being devoted to details and to an intelligent interpretation of the hymns etc. ...

"Choir Rules" exist from early 1900, and make interesting reading:

I   Members must belong to the Established Church and conform to its rules

Aylesford Choir, 1902

II   Attendance at the practice on Thursday and the Sunday services must not be less than at the rate of 75% per annum

III The election of new members or the dismissal of members shall be in the hands of the Vicar and Senior members

IV   All members must be in their places in the vestry five minutes before each service

V   The Vicar shall approve a senior member to take charge of the choir in his absence

VI   Quarterly meetings shall be held (of which due notice will be given) for this transaction of business.

Adopted Dec [year illegible, possibly 1902]
AJW Thorndike

In the Thorndike's time, additional musical support was provided by "half-a-dozen musicians from the Royal Engineers" (as recorded in the August 1952 article by Billy Wilson); bands had been used occasionally in the past, including the Royal Marines at Preston Hall *(PM, August 1865)*, and in the future, organ and choir were occasionally supplemented by other musicians, including on a regular basis by a music group, at the end of the 20th century (as detailed later).

Pertinent today, as we remember the centenary of the First World War, we note in the minutes of the vestry meeting of 5/4/1915, that the then vicar, Rev Sopwith, said that "... eight members of the choir were absent, which, in one sense he regretted, but at the same time he rejoiced to know that they had left to join the forces and were now serving their King and Country". Despite the ravages of the First World War – and the war memorial in the churchyard attests that Aylesford was no exception in the loss of so many during those years – the choir survived, reverting to a pattern familiar before the War. As Billy Wilson noted in his "Aylesford Fifty Years Ago" article in the September 1952 edition of the Parish Magazine:

> Another event which the choir looked for [*sic*] was the Annual Choirs' Festival of the Diocese of Rochester, which was held at the Cathedral. Most of the choirs in the Diocese took part. ...
> Another pleasure the choir had every year was the Annual Outing. This was a long-standing treat. I am unable to say when it began. In different years, all the popular seaside towns were visited, and very happy days enjoyed. So responsive to the appeal for subscriptions were the parishioners, that besides the railway fares being paid, dinners and teas were provided. These excursions continued until 1939, except for the years of the 1914 war. The Bellringers were entertained with a supper annually at Christmas time.

A choir visit to Crystal Palace on 27/6/1873 was recorded in the Parish Magazine of June 1873, as were Summer visits to Brighton, Herne Bay, Ramsgate, Hastings, Margate and Dover *(Parish Magazines (generally September) 1882-1900)*. In the June 1918 edition, we read of another outing:

> On Whit Monday Mr. Copley Hewitt took the choir boys and probationers, accompanied by the Vicar, to Maidstone, where, after a stroll round the County Town, they visited the "movies." Then followed a wonderful war-time tea, during which the thanks of the company were expressed to Mr. Hewitt for his kindness.

Aylesford Choir, sometime between 1915 and 1919

The Parish Magazine of June 1919 records:

> The choir. On December 23rd ... Mr Copley Hewitt took them [the boys of the choir] to Maidstone to see the pantomime ... When the performance was over, as there was more than an hour wait for the train, an adjournment was made to the Pictures ...

Some years later, in March 1932, Mr D Copley de Lisle Hewitt was to purchase the Friars (then known as Aylesford Place, as indicated on contemporary Ordnance Survey maps), after a fire had destroyed much of the property almost two years earlier; he began renovations there until his death in September 1941 *(Jim Sephton: "The Friars, Aylesford", pp57f)*

Women choristers join the choir

Women were first introduced into the choir during the time of Harold Moore, in 1947, initially on a temporary basis: "The girls robed in the Lady Chapel and at first did not take part in the procession." *(Ken Wells, letters 17/1/1988, quoting information from Elsie Wells, his sister-in-law, and one of the pioneer women choristers)*. Ken's brother, Len, in a conversation with the author (13/9/2002) said that Harold Moore realised that the number of boys in the choir was declining, and asked women to join in the performance of Stainer's "The Crucifixion" in 1947 (rehearsals started late 1946). Initially the women robed behind the organ (i.e. between the side of the organ and the Banks memorial), taking their places in the choir stalls (at that point in the chancel) whilst the boys and men processed in. The first time that the ladies processed in was for Len and Elsie Wells' wedding, on Saturday 22/9/1951.

Approval for the permanent admission of ladies to the choir finally occurred early in 1950, after Harold Moore highlighted the increasing difficulty of finding boys for the choir, and that "the church music was suffering accordingly" *(PCC Minutes, 7/2/1950)*.

By June 1947, the Parish Magazine records that

> The choir are to be sincerely congratulated on the completely unaccompanied services on Sunday, May 11th. A few months ago such services would have seemed impossible; however, the challenge of the organ being out of order owing to the installation of the electric blower, was met, faced and overcome splendidly. We hope to have more unaccompanied choir work.

On 30/10/1947, the choir became affiliated to the Royal School of Church Music: Whilst the annual membership fee of £2 is recorded as being paid on 31/10/1961, at some point later in the 1960s, membership lapsed. Affiliation was restored on 27/9/1973, since which time the choir has remained affiliated to the RSCM, utilising its training and awards schemes, the benefits of discounted music, and participation in Choirs Festival Services in Rochester, some 150 years after first taking part in them.

To assist with practices, Harold Moore began to use a harmonium, gifted to the church *(PM, December 1949)*:

> As announced at the Church Council Meeting, the Church has been the recipient of

a beautiful polished walnut harmonium in excellent condition, together with a stool to match, the gifts of Mrs. Janes, of Eccles. Our organist, Mr. H. F. Moore, says that he will find this instrument of great use during his rehearsals and choir practices.

Further assistance with choir practice was noted in the PCC minutes of 14/2/1955: "Request for the purchase of a tape recorder by Mr Moore (£30), to assist choir practice."

A "Minor Festival", involving several local Parish Church Choirs, took place in Aylesford late in 1952, and again on 3/10/1953 *(PM, September 1953)*, and whilst these provided encouragement for the choir, recruitment of new members continued to be an issue for Harold Moore: "I have appealed several times for ladies and boys, but without success. I know very well that there are those among the members of our congregation who could answer this appeal." *(PM, September 1954)*; a further appeal for new members ("boys … and adults in all parts") was made in the January 1960 edition of the Parish Magazine.

Aylesford Choir, 1976

AYLESFORD CHURCH OFFICE

Aylesford Choir, 1979

Aylesford Choir, c.1983

The choir remained in the Chancel even after the organ was moved into the main body of the church in 1965, but it became increasingly apparent by the mid-1970s that the choir, now comprising men, women, girls and boys, was becoming difficult to hear. Plans were put forward by Roy Burgess, the recently appointed new organist and choirmaster, to re-locate the choir in the nave, beneath the pulpit, just below the chancel steps. After an experimental move in 1976, the choir moved permanently in 1977 *(PM, February 1978)*.

A revised seating arrangement was advertised in the Parish Magazine of October 1978; and carried-out soon after, and it is this arrangement which exists to this day. With these plans, drawn-up by Roy Burgess, was the potential relocation of the organ console; however, as detailed below, this took nearly another 40 years to achieve!

The choir since 1985

Within the space of a year, Aylesford Choir appeared on national television twice, firstly when Harry Secombe and "Highway" came to Aylesford (May 1987), then for the charity fundraising programme "Telethon" (May 1988); a further TV appearance occurred on Advent Sunday, 1/12/1991, when TVS broadcast the Morning Service from Aylesford. This was not the first broadcast of the choir, however, as "Sunday Half Hour" had come from Preston Hall late in 1953 *(PM, January 1954)*, with the choir in attendance.

By 1988, when the first edition of this history was produced, the choir numbered around 40 members. Since then, in common with so many church choirs, numbers have eased: Currently there are just under 30 full-time choristers, with a further group of up to 10 Auxiliaries, who supplement the choir from time to time for the Easter oratorio, Carol Service and other major events (including the wedding of the author's daughter on 2/8/2014).

The author reported to the PCC of 24/4/1989 that "Mr Bill Linkstead will have been in the choir for 70 years by St Peterstide"; Bill remained in the choir for a few years after this, retiring in 1992 after 73 years' service, setting the record of the longest-serving chorister, one which will be hard to surpass! A music desk, which remains in very regular use, was purchased in Bill's memory. On it, the following inscription was placed:

> THANKSGIVING FOR BILL LINKSTEADS
> DEDICATED SERVICE TO THIS CHURCH

Church re-ordering plans in 1991 proposed moving the choir vestry to a position under the tower, with the font moving from there to the east of the organ; this was never carried out. Around this time, a brief experiment of moving the choir into the north aisle, below the Chancel steps, demonstrated that the optimal position of the choir was where it already was, in the south aisle.

Choir visits to other churches (including St George's Beckenham, Riverhead, Woodchurch and Dode) and annual Concerts were a feature of the choir's activity from the early 1990s (including Rochester Cathedral evensong on Whitsunday, 30/5/1993) until the mid-2000s, with a major concert in church on 7/7/2006 comprising the combined choirs of Aylesford, The Friars and Auxiliaries, with a small orchestra. Joint Choral Evensongs have also been undertaken over the last 20 years, mainly at Aylesford, with a number of different choirs (including Burham & Wouldham, East Malling, St Botolph's Northfleet, and St Mark's Plumsted). The choir has joined with the Friars choir for their Advent service each year for a number of years; further, joint Pentecost services switched between the Parish Church and The Friars over a similar period.

The style of worship in the Church of England has evolved significantly over its history, with particularly rapid liturgical change in the last 50 years providing added impetus to more informal styles of worship. Whilst many services still utilise traditional forms of worship, and traditional hymns, more modern hymns and worship songs are also occasionally used, and for a period of ten years (between October 1996 and December 2006), a music group was formed, led primarily by Helen Turner, for one Sunday service each month (the author played violin in this). The choir's repertoire is wide-ranging, from plainsong psalms (used on Ash Wednesday and Maundy Thursday) to contemporary anthems.

Choir outings have provided a social outlet for the choir since at least the early 20th century, and attendance at Choir Festivals at Rochester Cathedral (and as visitors to other churches, to sing Evensong) has strengthened the choir musically for even more years. Choir social activities (e.g. bowling in Maidstone or visits to the seaside) continue on an occasional basis, and from the early 1980s until 2000, a very successful weekend away provided both musical training and social interaction for the choir: Initially these were held at a retreat house in Chislehurst; by 1986 they were being held at a retreat house in Westgate-on-Sea, and then for three years from 1996, camping at Ashburnham (Sussex); rising costs prevented these from continuing.

The choir's affiliation to the Royal School of Church Music (RSCM) has provided a structure for training, particularly for the Junior Choir, and the opportunity to continue the very long tradition of attending Choral Festival Services at Rochester Cathedral. A number of the current choir have gained Bronze, Silver or Gold awards, externally examined by the RSCM. Since 2001, Junior Choir leaders (initially Christopher Haydon and Janet McConnell) took on responsibility for the training of the Junior Choir. In 2005 Helen Turner became Junior Choir leader (as well as continuing as assistant organist), and is now assisted in

this role by others including Lizzie Cook (who, as daughter of the organist (and author), is maintaining family choral traditions!)

As well as appearing on television, as noted above, the choir has also been on radio, and recorded a CD; a number of recordings of the choir concerts were made by Ken Drury, a friend of the author and professional sound engineer. A list of these choir TV and radio appearances and some of the recordings, together with recordings of the organ, is provided in Appendix N.

Auxiliary choir

The current necessity of Auxiliary singers has been noted above, supplementing the ongoing recruitment drive for permanent Choristers. This is not a new phenomenon: As early as 1872, the Harvest Evening Service (29/9/1872) the choir was "augmented by some of the experienced singers in the congregation ..." *(PM, October 1872)*; the Parish Magazines of February 1947 and April 1950 advertised performances of Stainer's "The Crucifixion", with "Augmented Choir & Soloists", and an "augmented choir" was thanked for the Musical Service of 27/11/1947 *(PM, January 1948)*.

Bells and handbells

The focus of this history is on the organ and choir, as they are inextricably linked in the musical ministry of any church. However, mention must be made of the work of the bellringers (under the current leadership of Darren Elphick), whose very public display of music has been heard across Aylesford for centuries: A short history of the bells at Aylesford Church was produced as a separate booklet in 2005-6, following the restoration of five of the eight bells. These bells are also playable as a "carillon" by a single player, from a cabinet at the foot of the tower. For many years, this was used before and after Sunday afternoon services by Bill Linkstead: It is to be hoped that the gentle and prayerful ringing of the bells in this way will once again become a regular part of our bell ringing.

In recent years, a band of hand bell ringers have also provided musical input to the Christmas Carol and Easter Morning services, as well as the Harvest Supper, led by Gordon Hunt.

Part 3: 1965–Present

The early 1960s – The Forster & Andrews organ in need of work as it reaches its 100th anniversary

Background to the 1965 rebuild

Within sixteen years of the works undertaken on the organ in 1947, it became clear that major work was necessary to maintain the viability of the organ for the future: "Mr Moore stated that the action of the organ continued to deteriorate. He undertook to get in touch with Mr Harvey for a report" *(PCC Minutes, 25/3/1963)*. An "Organ Restoration Fund" was opened by the PCC *(14/10/1963 meeting)*, but by the PCC meeting of 29/10/1963 a second threat to the organ had materialised: An electronic organ was to be temporarily installed "to enable opinions on such an organ to be formulated". On a visit to the church for Evensong on 17/11/1963, Frank A Oakley expressed his horror at finding the electronic organ was being tested and compared with the existing pipe organ. In a long article *(PM, January 1964)*, he concludes that

> Our old pipe organ … can be restored, modernised, and rebuilt (and none of its superb craftsmanship be lost) … We owe it to the craftsmen who built this organ. They have provided us with a fine instrument, worthy of every penny we must spend on it to put it in good condition.

By the time the article was published, the PCC had received an offer of an interest-free loan of up to £2,000 for seven years, conditional on the pipe organ being restored *(PCC Minutes 15/12/1963)*; accordingly the PCC abandoned the purchase of an electronic organ, and backed the rebuilding of the existing organ.

It is not clear what Harvey's view of the proposed work was, as he did not tender a formal quotation: The scale of the proposed work is likely to have been too great for him to contemplate, and as noted above, it seems almost certain that he was entering retirement. Quotations were requested by Harold Moore from Dickinson of Truro and NP Mander Ltd of London. The Manders assessment of the condition of, and options for, the organ was produced on 6/5/1963: The action, largely untouched since 1865, was "very worn, very noisy", with the soundboard pallets "very hard". The 1947 B.O.B. blower was also considered "fairly noisy". Whilst indicating the date "1879" on initial survey (derived from the date plate on the case), their detailed report erroneously stated that "This organ was build [*sic*] in 1859", but correctly noted that it had "had no renewal to action since." Manders recommended "new electric action", "a new Discus Blower", and the fitting of a new console (although not explicitly a detached console – a misunderstanding between Manders and Harold Moore, which took over a year to surface).

The PCC deemed a complete rebuild to be the only viable option, together with a relocation of the organ to another part of the church (first suggested in the fabric report of 1943): The impact of the organ in the North Aisle Chancel gave rise to acoustic issues (see Appendix M), blocked a great deal of light from the east end of the church and prevented the chancel being used as a chapel. The PCC Meeting of 31/5/1964 opted for a position in the north west corner of the church, behind the vestry door, but by the meeting of 26/8/1964 (and following negotiations with the diocese), this had reverted to the north wall position which it now occupies. In that position, the Brassey Memorial window would not be obscured.

It was also noted in the 31/5/1964 Meeting that the work would commence "after Christmas 1964, for completion before Easter, 1965"; in the event, it was early June 1965 before the re-opening – a delay which was to be repeated 50 years later at the next major rebuild, proving again that the art of organ building can rarely be time constrained!

The work and plans were coordinated, once again, by Harold Moore; the PCC awarded the contract to the Hackney firm of NP Mander Ltd on the basis of them being "better known … and better situated." *(PCC Minutes, 4/3/1964)*; placing the order for the work, though, would need to await the arrival of the new vicar. Even after the order was confirmed, in a letter from Harold Moore to NP Mander on 16/12/1963, detailed discussions to reach an agreed specification and scope of works continued for almost a year before the work was finally agreed and started; even then, changes were made as the work actually progressed.

Gary Tollerfield was appointed Chairman of the Appeals Committee, which organised pipe shares, old newspaper collections, a series of concerts and recitals, and a photographic exhibition on 8/10/1964, sponsored by Kodak, in the Corn Exchange, Maidstone. The choir also pledged to raise £500 of the almost £4,000 required, and Harold Moore went without his organist's salary for one year, and then refused to have it increased.

Planning the 1965 rebuild

Manders noted that the church did not wish the organ to occupy any more space than it currently did, and proposed moving the organ elsewhere in the church, or rebuilding it on a raised platform. They also provided an initial scheme, which would have moved the Great Clarionet 8' onto the Great soundboard in place of the Harmonic Flute 4' (which would have been discarded), retaining the Swell division without any alterations, and creating two Pedal units, one for the Bourdon 16' (extended to Flute 8' and Flute 4'), and the other comprising an Octave 8' and Fifteenth 4', discarding the bottom octave of the Open Diapason 16' rank altogether (12 large wooden pipes inside the organ).

In the 16/12/1963 letter confirming the order with NP Mander, Harold Moore reproduced the Dickinson recommended specification, in order to assist resolution of some of the Mander suggestions which Harold Moore disagreed with. Whilst Harold Moore agreed to the removal of the Great Clarionet 8' (and therefore the retention of the Great Harmonic Flute 4'), he disagreed with the need to remove the Pedal Open Diapason 16', as "no other builder has found anything against retaining it." With the Great Trumpet 8' still within the specification, Harold Moore would doubtless have realised that the loss of the Clarionet 8' would be far less impacting in terms of the organ's tonal flexibility than the loss of the 4' Flute.

In common with the Mander specification, Dickinson proposed the retention of the Swell division without alteration, but recommended replacing the Great Clarionet 8' with a 3 rank Mixture; he took a very different view of how to deal with the Pedal division, retaining the existing stops, but also extending the Bourdon 16' to create a Bass Flute 8', and creating an Acoustic Bass 32' from the Open Diapason 16'.

Manders responded with a revised specification on 30/1/1964: The Great Clarionet 8' and Harmonic Flute 4' were to go (although handwritten notes then state "Nas Flute 4 in place of Harmonic"), and a 3 rank Mixture would replace the Bourdon 16' on the Swell (where it "would be more effective"). The Pedal Open Diapason 16' was now retained in the scheme, but renamed as Open Wood 16', and it's first extension (previously Principal 8') as Octave 8'. They also dismissed the idea of an Acoustic 32":

"We do not favour a 'phoney' 32 ft. derived from the existing pipework. It can never be in tune and is quite offensive under certain circumstances." The new console was again quoted as part of this specification, although in a letter from Manders to Harold Moore dated 24/9/1964 we read: "I think there is a little misunderstanding concerning the console ... With the moving of the organ we intended the console to go with it. A detached console is something for which we have never specifically quoted."

By 6/10/1964, an "Agreed Specification" had finally been reached, with the Great losing the Clarionet 8', and having the Harmonic Flute 4' substituted by a Nason Flute 4', the Pedal division having two 16.8.4 units based on the Open Diapason (now called Open Wood) and Bourdon, and the Swell having a 3 rank Mixture in place of the Lieblich Bourdon 16'; the Swell Flute d'Amour 8' was also to be revoiced as a Viol d'Amour 8'. Harold Moore looked to increasing the range of couplers. He requested two sets of three thumb pistons which became part of the final specification and for these to be duplicated by toe pistons, which did not.

A listing of the order of the stop tabs on the console stop tab rail was provided on 18/1/1965, a few weeks after the commencement of the works, which indicates that by then agreement had been reached to provide a detached console, at an additional cost of £340. The listing indicates that the planned re-voicing of the Swell Flute d'Amour would not occur, although the Great listing still includes a "Clarinet 8'" [sic] (i.e. Clarionet 8') at the expense of the Harmonic or Nason Flute 4': This must be an error by Manders, as the Nason Flute 4' was an early agreement, and new pipework would have already have been made; the 'as built' specification had no Clarionet 8', but did include the Nason Flute 4'.

❋❋

NP Mander, organ builders

Noel Mander came from a family of organ builders dating back to the 18th century: In 1936, he founded Mander Organs, expanding rapidly in the late 1940s, undertaking the reconstruction of many organs which had been damaged in the Second World War. Over the following years, the firm continued to expand, taking on the rebuilding of some high profile organs in the UK (including St Paul's Cathedral, London (1972-77, and subsequently), and Rochester Cathedral (1989)), as well as numerous Parish

Church organs, including the Forster & Andrews organ at Aylesford, in 1965.

Mander's expansion continued into the Middle East, America and Africa; now, under the Directorship of Noel Mander's son, John, the firm has extended their works further into Japan, Australia, New Zealand and Scandinavia. The Mander Organ works continue to be located in the Bethnal Green area of East London, although the tuning side of the business was sold-off in 2002 to David Wintle, the tuner of Aylesford's organ since 1987, but continues to use the Mander name (NP Mander (Tunings) Ltd).

Noel Mander, NP Mander (organ builders)

1965 – The Forster & Andrews organ modernised

Changes within the organ

Work on modernising the organ commenced immediately after Christmas 1964, and was to continue for six months.

Whilst Manders were clear that the organ was not to occupy any more space, the introduction of a detached console meant that the front of the organ could be further forwards than would have been the case had the console remained integrated into the organ. The abortive attempt to move the organ back to the west wall dictated a north aisle position, and with the front of the organ lined-up with the tiled aisle path, this allowed 2' (0.61m) additional space at the rear in addition to some space within the reveal of the middle window of the north aisle, now obscured (although not blocked-up) by the organ.

This additional 32½ sq ft (2.99 sq m) of space was utilised to provide a passageway at the back of the organ, with doors either end, to facilitate maintenance; it also housed the new blowing plant and rectifier. At a higher level, access to the rear of the Swell box was made by inserting two removable panels into the bottom half of the back wall of the box; this was reached by a new passage board, which also provided access to the Pedal extension pipework located on off-note chests placed within the window area. Rear maintenance access to the Swell box was essential to facilitate tuning the new Swell Mixture stop.

In order to blend the additional space at the back of the organ into the original, Manders extended the cornice on the north side of the case, created two new pillars against the north wall, and edged the original back pillars to match those at the front. The cornice was not extended on the south side of the organ, as this was less visible; it has also preserved the historical evidence of the cornice cut-out, noted earlier, which confirms the organ's previous North Aisle Chancel position against the Milner memorial. Inside, the lower pipes of the Pedal Bourdon 16' which had been supported by the wall were now braced to the wall across the newly-created space at the rear of the organ.

Included in the Pedal extensions were 12 reused pipes discarded from the Swell Lieblich Bourdon 16', to make the Fifteenth 4' (derived from the Open Wood 16', and now reverted to its original naming of Open Diapason 16'). The 8' and 4' Flute extensions of unit 2 (based on the Pedal Bourdon 16') were undertaken using new pipework.

The work also included the installation of a new Watkins and Watkins 'Discus' blower. On 6/4/1965, some way through the works, Manders wrote to Harold Moore, indicating that "the construction of the [Swell] soundboard is such that it is impossible to get the [Mixture] pipes standing, or to alter it to let them stand. I have no alternative, therefore, than to make the mixture stop at Tenor C"; in consequence, the Mixture was constructed without a bottom octave; modern technology finally allowed this to be achieved in the 2015 rebuild. During the dismantling of the organ in 2014, it was noted that some pipes of the Swell Oboe 8' had suffered impact damage from the Swell shutters, which themselves had been carved in places to prevent this happening; closer inspection revealed that the entire Swell soundboard appears to have been moved forwards slightly in the 1965 rebuild, in order to accommodate the Mixture pipework, and this was the cause of the damage to the Oboe.

On-site work was undertaken by Harold Newman of Manders, and other work (including soundboard renovation and some revoicing) was carried out in Mander's workshops.

The final contract price was £3,933.00: A loan of £1,800 from an anonymous Parishioner, referred to as "Agricola", together with some initial fundraising (around

£200 by May 1965), had enabled the work to commence. By May 1966, £1,500 had been raised, leaving a £700 gap in funding, and the outstanding loan of £1,800. The May 1965 edition of the Parish Magazine reported that a total of £2,120 was still outstanding or to be repaid to the "Agricola Trust", which had been set-up to use the repaid loan to support Ministry training in Aylesford and Wouldham. By March 1970, the loan to "Agricola" remained outstanding, but the balance of the costs had been covered. The initial seven year term of this loan would suggest that it would have finally been repaid in 1971: This view is supported by the vicar's annual report presented on 15/2/1972, which states, "A large deficit has been wiped off from the account books"; further, the accounts for the year ending 31/12/1973 show year end 1972 & 1973, with no reference to this loan.

The restoration of the organ was complete by Whitsunday, 6th June 1965. The north windows of the Lady Chapel, blocked since 1879, were restored in 1966, funded by the Brassey Trust.

The specification after the 1965 rebuild is detailed on the following page.

The Mander Nason Flute 4' from the Aylesford organ now also exists in a 'virtual' world: Having sampled the organ in April 2002, Wyvern Organs now regularly use this stop in their custom-built electronic organs.

1965 re-opening concerts and recitals

An initial concert was held on Wednesday 2/6/1965, shortly before the organ was complete. During this concert, Noel Mander gave a talk on 'Organ Building', a recording of which still exists.

The opening recital was given by Dr Robert Ashfield (organist of Rochester Cathedral) on Friday 2/7/1965. A further recital was given by Harry Gabb (of Her Majesty's Chapels Royal, and assistant organist at St Paul's Cathedral) on Friday 17/9/1965: Harry Gabb had previously been sub-organist at St Paul's Cathedral, then organist at Llandaff Cathedral; his invitation to play at

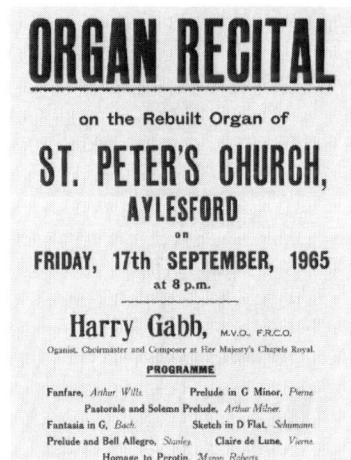

ORGAN RECITAL

on the Rebuilt Organ of

ST. PETER'S CHURCH,
AYLESFORD
on

FRIDAY, 17th SEPTEMBER, 1965
at 8 p.m.

Harry Gabb, M.V.O. F.R.C.O.

Organist, Choirmaster and Composer at Her Majesty's Chapels Royal.

PROGRAMME

Fanfare, *Arthur Wills*	Prelude in G Minor, *Pierne*
Pastorale and Solemn Prelude, *Arthur Milner*	
Fantasia in G, *Bach*	Sketch in D Flat, *Schumann*
Prelude and Bell Allegro, *Stanley*	Claire de Lune, *Vierne*
Homage to Perotin, *Myron Roberts*	

Poster from one of the opening recitals after the 1965 rebuild

1965 SPECIFICATION
NP Mander Ltd

Compass: Manuals CC - g3, 56 note.
Pedals CCC - F, 30 note.
Electric Action, 3" wind.

Great

1.	Open Diapason	8'
2.	Stopt Diapason	8'
3.	Dulciana	8'
4.	Principal	4'
5.	Nason Flute	4'
6.	Twelfth	2 ⅔'
7.	Fifteenth	2'
8.	Trumpet	8'

Pedal

(Radiating & concave, Willis pattern)

16.	Open Wood	16'
17.	Bourdon	16'
18.	Octave	8'
19.	Flute	8'
20.	Fifteenth	4'
21.	Flute	4'

Notes:

5 replaced 4' Harmonic Flute.
13 new (replaced 16' Leiblich Bourdon).
16 & 18 renamed (only bottom octave of 16 is wood).
18 & 20 from 16.
19 & 21 from 17-24 new pipes on 19 & 21 from discarded 16' Swell Bourdon.
30 & 31 new, as part of detached console.
New detached console (Mander).
Replacement electric blower.

Swell (enclosed)

9.	Open Diapason	8'
10.	Flûte d'Amour	8'
	(TC, CC-BB from No 10)	8'
11.	Principal	4'
12.	III rk Mixture (TC)	III
	15.19.22	
13.	Principal	4'
14.	Cornopean	8'
15.	Oboe	8'

Accessories

22. Swell to Great
23. Swell Oct. to Great
24. Swell Sub Oct to Gt.
25. Swell to Pedals
26. Great to Pedals
27. Swell Octave
28. Swell Sub Octave
29. 3 adjustable combination thumb pistons to each manual
30. 2 reversible pistons for 22 & 26
31. Balanced Swell pedal
    Switch selectable double-touch tab stops (for cancellation)

(1012 pipes)

Aylesford was as a result of a direct approach by Noel Mander, as confirmed in a letter to Gary Tollerfield from St James's Palace on 27/5/1965. In all, some six recitals took place over a seven-month period, as recorded by the Kent Messenger.

After Harold Moore's death in 1969, a brass memorial plate was placed on the organ case to commemorate the immense amount of work undertaken by him to save and restore this fine instrument:

In memory of HAROLD MOORE
ORGANIST AND CHOIRMASTER 1946 – 1969
under whose direction this organ was restored and moved from the chancel.

The Mander console

The finally agreed works ("as built") included the provision of a detached console, linked to the organ by multi-core low voltage electrical cables. Almost certainly for reasons of economy (as the additional costs for a detached console were only agreed to very late in the contract negotiations), Manders provided a two manual and pedals console with stop and coupler tabs (rather than the more traditional draw stops knobs), three switch selectable thumb pistons to each manual, and reversible thumb pistons for Swell to Great and Great to Pedal. In common with the design of many small Mander consoles at the time, the closed console cover enabled the manuals to be seen through two perspex windows: This appearance gave rise to term "fish fryer console", by which these Mander consoles were affectionately known.

With the choir still occupying the chancel choir stalls, the console was placed behind the north choir stalls, in the south of the Lady Chapel. To accommodate this, iron railings were removed from between the two central piers of the chancel. PCC minutes from the time simply consider removing the railings "for scrap", although they may have gone to the 'Little Gem' pub in the village *(Jim Sephton, Aylesford Society Journal, Vol. 1 No 3, December 1994, p.8)*; other sources state that the balcony ironwork in the Little Gem came "from the stage of an old barn at the vicarage where Dame Sybil Thorndike acted when her father was vicar of Aylesford" *(Alan McCrerie, "Knowing Aylesford", p.4)*, so there is some uncertainty here.

The rationale behind the positioning of the console in the Lady Chapel behind the choir disappeared in 1977 when the choir moved into the Nave; it was to take almost

Tuning the pipes on the re-built organ in St. Peter's Church, Aylesford. Story on page

Mr. H. Newman regulating the pipework at the new console, which is now sited by the choir.

Church aims high for organ facelift

A HUNDRED years ago, one December day, the barrel organ at St. Peter's Church, Aylesford, was replaced by a fine new organ. The cost — a modest £270.

And that same instrument has served St. Peter's since its installation without a single major overhaul.

Now, a few months before its hundredth anniversary, the organ is being treated to £3,800 facelift, which has re-established its reputation as one of the finest parish church organs in the county.

Mr. Gary F. Tollerfield, chairman of the Organ Fund Raising Committee is proceeding with a number of schemes to help pay for the restoration.

The schemes are ambitious, but so far the results have been encouraging. Over £1,100 has already been raised. But a further £2,700 must be found to cover the cost of the work.

A waste paper scheme has raised £200, and much of the rest has been raised by a pipe share card scheme.

This involves filling a special card with saving stamps, which when full (value £1) can be exchanged for a certificate.

Wednesday night saw the first of six recitals planned for the next seven months.

It featured James Bates, a professional London counter-tenor, Edward Bower (tenor), and Allison Merry (Mezzo-Soprano).

Andrew Jones, leader of the Kent Youth Orchestra, performed on violin and on piano, and Mr. N. P. Mander gave a talk on organ building.

The inaugural organ recital will be given by Dr. Robert Ashfield on July 2.

Dates and programmes have yet to be fixed for the other organ recitals, but it is hoped Dr. Harry Gabb, Chapels Royal and assistant to St. Pauls, and Margaret Cobb, St. Lawrence Jewry next Guildhall.

Apart from these professional concerts, a mammoth slide competition is planned for October.

It will be advertised throughout Kent, and Kodak have agreed to judge the winning entries. The competition will be open to all, and it is hoped that over 5,000 slides will be submitted.

"We're aiming high" says Mr. Tollerfield, "and we're risking quite a bit. But we think the results of all our campaigns will justify our methods".

The 1965 rebuild, as reported by the Kent Messenger

40 years for the resultant remoteness of the organist to be resolved, as described more fully later.

The 1965 works reviewed

It is unclear why the Great Harmonic Flute 4' was replaced by a similar pitched Nason Flute, which is tonally uncharacteristic of Forster & Andrews' work (although pleasant in its own right); still less clear is why both Pedal stops were extended to 4', other than this was popular at the time. The effectiveness of the new Mixture stop was compromised by its being buried at the back of the Swell box, rather than being re-introduced further forwards (and unenclosed) onto the Great division as suggested by Dickinson. All that said though, the 1965 work was undertaken to the highest standards, and ensured that the organ was retained and preserved for another generation: Most of the soundboard pallets, when uncovered nearly 50 years later, were found to be in excellent condition.

1965 to 2015 – The Forster & Andrews organ through times of liturgical change

1965 to 1987

The organ remained in the care of NP Mander Ltd until R Beddoes' last tuning visit on 21/3/1977. The tuning visits had been reduced to two per year by October 1974 (following a financial crisis within the church), at a cost of £16.32 + 8% VAT each. As a consequence of concerns over these costs by the Treasurer and PCC, the local firm of Wood Brown Ltd were engaged to tune and maintain the organ, their first visit being on 29/6/1977; Wood Brown's Manager, Terry Wood, had worked for Manders between February and July 1961. Manders expressed their concern at losing this contract in two letters, dated 2/10/1975 and 27/7/1978; in the former, they reminded C A Watt, the treasurer, of the 20 year guarantee on the new action, which would be invalidated if anyone other than Manders maintained the organ.

In mid-1980, the middle B of the Nason Flute 4', plus the top G# and A of the Pedal Fifteenth 4', went missing. These were replaced by Wood Brown, who also placed a lock on the organ to prevent this happening again.

Roy Burgess highlighted to the PCC in 1981 that a clean and overhaul was "now due" *(PCC Minutes, 23/3/1981)*. Dirt falling into the Organ from the roof, and other problems including sticking sliders, confirmed by 1986 that a cleaning and overhaul was necessary. Part of the proposed work was to construct a more permanent and effective canopy over the Trumpet rank, as this stop was prone to be most affected by the dirt – the pipes are open-topped and conical.

Four organ builders were approached to tender for the work: NP Mander Ltd; Hill, Norman and Beard (who had taken over Forster and Andrews in 1956); Ron Parratt of Rochester (who in 1973 had assisted the move of the King Street Maidstone organ to Detling church); and Wood Brown Ltd. The contract was awarded to Manders, restoring their care of the instrument once again. The last visit of Wood Brown was on 7/3/1987.

Consideration was given to adding a Salicional 8' to the Great, as a balance to the very full Diapason chorus, typical of Forster and Andrews organs. Manders were not in favour of this, not least due to space constraints, although they did provide a quotation for the work, and identified some second-hand pipework to reduce costs. Whilst the addition of the Great Salicional 8' was not progressed, mainly to contain costs, other tonal alterations were made, to improve the overall balance of the instrument and improve its flexibility. The Pedal Bourdon 16' (and extensions) was re-voiced to provide a quieter tone in contrast to the Open Wood 16' – the Bourdon had been a typically English full-toned stop, too loud for quiet manual registration; the Swell Oboe 8' was re-voiced to become a better solo stop; the Great Trumpet 8' was re-voiced to provide a more consistent tone; and a Tremulant was added to the Swell to provide greater variety of tone on the quieter registrations.

As well as the proposed Salicional, the contract also included costs for screwing and pegging the soundboards, which was found not to be necessary; it also included moving the console from the Lady Chapel to the north aisle behind the choir stalls (with the expectation that a platform would be in place in time for the console to be moved); again, this element of the works was not carried out. The scope of the works also included attending to damaged pipework and freeing sticking sliders.

As a consequence of all the changes, the original contract price of £4,585 plus 15% VAT reduced to a final cost of £3,946.80 including VAT, £2,000 of which was paid as a grant by the Brassey Trust.

During the works, Manders provided a small temporary 2 manual and pedals organ. The work commenced on Tuesday 11th August 1987, and was completed during the first week of September. David Wintle, of Manders, worked on site, with pipework for revoicing being returned to Manders' workshops.

The specification after the 1987 work can be seen overleaf.

Ranks wholly or partially original have been indicated in the specification, by way of reference.

The organ since 1987

As a separate piece of work to the Manders 1987 overhaul, the blower was repaired and serviced by V Hobbs, engineer with Watkins and Watson, on 30/3/1987, at a cost of £57.50 including 15% VAT. Regular oiling of the blower has occurred since, but at some point a further overhaul will become necessary.

Following the 1987 rebuild, the organ was generally very reliable, but there were signs from time to time that work would eventually need to be done: A sticking Swell slider (Cornopean 8'), a cyphering Pedal Open 16' case pipe, increasing tonal irregularity particularly in the Swell Oboe 8' and Great Trumpet 8' stops, occasional issues with one or two of the console stop tabs, as well as the general accumulation of dirt over the years. More significant though was the appreciation that almost all of the wiring dated from 1965.

No-one dared move the transmission wiring loom which linked the console to the organ for fear of it fracturing and thus causing total failure, and this was the main reason that the console remained in the Lady Chapel for so long. A modern transmission system (data cable and multiplexing units) was the only way forwards. With a detached console, restoring the mechanical tracker action from pre-1965 was no longer feasible, and would have been both prohibitively expensive and difficult to justify.

A new mains electrical supply was provided to the console early in 1996, following electrical problems during 1995; this was undertaken by Bren Wards Ltd (via Priory Contract Services), at a cost of £1,850.63 including 17½% VAT. Further electrical issues occurred on 19/12/1996, when the organ stopped working; Adam Rawlinson (Priory Contract Services and a member of the choir) identified that a fuse had blown on the

1987 SPECIFICATION
NP Mander Ltd

Compass: Manuals CC - g3, 56 note.
Pedals CCC - F, 30 note.
Electric Action, 3" wind.

Great

1.	Open Diapason *	8'
2.	Stopt Diapason *	8'
3.	Dulciana *	8'
4.	Principal *	4'
5.	Nason Flute	4'
6.	Twelfth *	2 2/3'
7.	Fifteenth *	2'
8.	Trumpet	8'

Swell (enclosed)

9.	Open Diapason +	8'
10.	Stopt Diapason *	8'
11.	Flûte d'Amour +	8'
	(TC, CC-BB from No 10)	
12.	Principal *	4'
13.	III rk Mixture (TC)	III
	15.19.22	
14.	Cornopean +	8'
15.	Oboe +	8'

Pedal
(RCO, Willis pattern)

16.	Open Wood **	16'
17.	Bourdon *	16'
18.	Octave ++	8'
19.	Flute +	8'
20.	Fifteenth ++	4'
21.	Flute +	4'

Accessories

22. Swell to Great
23. Swell Oct. to Great
24. Swell Sub Oct to Gt.
25. Swell to Pedals
26. Great to Pedals
27. Swell Octave
28. Swell Sub Octave
29. 3 adjustable combination thumb
    pistons to each manual
30. 2 reversible pistons for 22 & 26
31. Swell Tremulant
32. Balanced Swell pedal
    Switch selectable double-touch tab
    stops (for cancellation)

(1012 pipes)

Notes:

31 new.
18 & 20 from 16.
19 & 21 from 17.
8, 5, 17, 19 & 21 revoiced.
Detached console, Mander.

F & A 1865 pipework:
Wholly [*]; partially [+]
F & A 1879 pipework:
Wholly [**]; partially [++]

240V side of the rectifier. This was replaced with new 5A anti-surge fuse. However, these incidents served to indicate that the reliability of the organ electrics was becoming a cause for concern, and would need to be addressed in the next organ restoration.

Repairs to the church late in 1987 (following storm damage in October 1987) necessitated the covering of the organ, to prevent dirt and debris falling into the organ: The cost, including re-tuning once the covering was removed, was £741.75 including 15% VAT. The organ was covered-up again after Easter 1995, whilst repairs to the interior of the church took place, as identified during the quinquennial inspection.

Although Aylesford church is not generally well known for its good heating, there have been occasions when higher temperatures have caused issues, usually in the winter when the air is also dry. The combination of higher temperature and dry air causes wood and leather to dry out and wind leakage to occur. Insufficient wind to support full organ was first noted in early 1997, and again in early 1999, early 2000, and early 2001; Steve Bayley of FH Browne believes these issues are most likely to have resulted from the temperature and dryness combination. David Wintle's notes on the tuning visit of 30/4/2001 support this: The irregular (and often excessive) church heating was the cause of issues for the organ. Correspondence between the organist and vicar (Simon Tillotson), especially after a cypher appeared on 6/5/2002, resulted in the church heating controls being rectified and the organ settling down again. It now also seems possible that the sticking Swell Cornopean 8' slide, first noted on 11/3/1999, was also exacerbated by these heating issues: This was repaired by Manders on 13-14/9/1999, at a cost of £519.94 including 17½% VAT, and paid for by Stan Joyner (father of Mary Smelt, a long-term chorister and wife of John Smelt, one of the Readers).

It was also clear that the deteriorating insulation around the large heating pipes which ran through the back of the organ were not helping either, so the re-lagging of these was proposed for the next rebuild works. In the event, they were undertaken separately in March 2012, by Lee Crawley (Medway Insulations Ltd), at no cost to the church.

Creature-comforts of the 20th century had finally reached Aylesford Church, and the increasing amount of carpet in the church had a negative impact on the effectiveness of the organ to provide a clear and bright lead, particularly when the church was full. The acoustics of Aylesford church are fairly dry, and what little resonance there had been in the building in 1865 when the organ was built (mainly from stone floors and Victorian floor tiles) was now severely compromised. An approach was needed to restore the effectiveness of the organ. On 6/5/2002, the author e-mailed Simon Tillotson (vicar) to highlight a number of factors including the need to address the reduction in power of the organ, particularly with a full church, due to the increasing amount of carpeting. It was also suggested that a major overhaul of the organ would soon be necessary, potentially around 2007.

Between the rebuilds of 1987 and 2015, tuning and general maintenance were carried out twice yearly by David Wintle of NP Mander (latterly trading as NP Mander Tunings Ltd). David ensured that anything which could be done to keep the organ working well was done, and highlighted any concerns so that action could be taken. As organist, I would take this opportunity to express a deep gratitude to David (and to Pam (his wife) and Chris (his son), who both assisted) for an excellent job carried out over nearly 30 years: That there was never cause to bring David back to do any corrective work is testament to the quality of the tuning and maintenance work carried out each visit.

Some changes in the wider world almost had an impact on the organ: The first of these concerned increased metrication, particularly with the Units of Measurement Regulations 1994. The following comment was recorded in the tuning book by the author (in jest) in September 1995: "I suppose we'll have to refer to the Gt 2.436m Stopt from now on …!". David Wintle entered into the spirit with the response, "Organ not to be used after 1st Oct until new metric "EEC Stop tabs" have been fitted …". Fortunately, organ stop designations (8', 4' etc) have not been affected by metrication! Then, just as work for the latest restoration was being planned in 2006, the EU Directives on Hazardous Substances (RoHS) were coming into force, which for a while threatened the maintenance of pipe organs, as their lead content far exceeded the new legal standards. Fortunately sense prevailed, and organs were made exempt. Richard Morrison, in "The Times" of 18/3/2006, commented that he doubted there had been a single instance of a person being poisoned by a pipe organ, whereas he knew of many accidents involving organ stools, overweight organists and alcohol, and "many organists whose performances should be banned on public health grounds"!

Following a briefing to the PCC in October 2005 (where costs were expected to be around £23,000), an Organ Overhaul Steering Committee (OOSC) was formed the following month, but a year later (and with just £1,000 raised towards costs) the committee was temporarily suspended, to allow a focus on the building of new toilet and kitchenette facilities in church. However, an initial survey on the organ was conducted by Mander Tunings on 6/1/2006, which noted (amongst other things) that the organ was quite dirty: Eight years later (when the organ was finally dismantled), the amount of dirt and cobwebs had increased to such an extent that Steve Bayley (FH Browne) commented that it was one of the dirtiest organ he'd worked on! Paul Isom (Diocesan Organ Advisor (DOA) for Rochester) produced a report on 26/5/2006, and quotations for the works were received from Martin K Cross and FH Browne.

The organ project took a 'back seat' whilst the "Flush Fund" raised some £75,000, mainly from within the church, and included the then vicar, Rev. Simon Tillotson, dragging a toilet around the parish for people to throw in a penny (or, hopefully, more); the provision of a toilet had apparently been talked about since early in the 20th century! With the new facilities completed, the new vicar, Rev. Chris van Straaten, brought the focus back onto the organ in December 2009. A small group was formed to drive the project forwards, comprising Chris van Straaten (vicar), Alan Longmuir (churchwarden), Robin Turner (assistant organist's husband) and Michael Keays (organist).

Scope of work for the 2015 rebuild

The scope of the work was initially to undertake just a cleaning and rewiring of the organ, and to make whatever tonal enhancements were possible with the existing pipework, to counteract the effects of the carpet which was laid in the church in the 1990s. What became clear, though, when discussing this with Paul Isom, the Diocesan Organ Advisor (DOA), was that the approach to 'brightening' the organ was unlikely to be completely successful; rather, we should look at reinstating a Great Mixture, which had been removed in 1894. The logical position for this restored rank was in its original place on the Great soundboard, i.e., where the Trumpet had been installed, and indeed when the upper boards were lifted in 2014, the original Mixture slide was still present in the soundboard. The reinstatement of a Great Mixture necessitated the relocation of the Trumpet 8' on its own off-note chests, which allowed further extensions to create brightness (Clarion 4') and a much needed Pedal reed (Trombone 16'), by extending the Trumpet 8' an octave at each end of its compass. Although tight, the additional space created at the back of the organ for the 1965 rebuild allowed these changes to be accommodated.

A further recommended enhancement was the completion of the 1965 Swell Mixture, which had only been built down to Tenor C; completing the bottom octave was desirable and it was now feasible.

The Mander console, re-worked FH Browne, 2015. Note the additional thumb and toe pistons, and memories controller (right of manuals)

The initial proposed specification for the composition of the Great Mixture was very high, but after intervention from the DOA, this was revised to the final 15.19.22, which is both in keeping with the rest of the instrument, and the most likely composition of the original Forster & Andrews pipework. Following the recommendation of Paul Hale (Rector Chori at Southwell Minster, and former DOA for Rochester), the bottom octave of the Great Mixture was raised slightly higher, to 19.22.26. The break points of the Swell and Great Mixtures (i.e. the point on the keyboard where the Mixtures drop one harmonic to lower pitches) differs between Swell and Great, so that it is less apparent to the listener when both Mixtures are in use.

In order to prepare for the next 50 years, work was commissioned on the organ to address the following:

- General cleaning (the organ was extremely dirty)

- Re-electrification (most of the wiring was 50 years old, and cotton covered on the low voltage side)

- Tonal improvements (to counter the effect of excessive carpeting in the church, also noted in the DOA's report, to restore some brightness to the organ)

- Console refurbishment (to utilise modern computer technology for transmission between console and organ, and for the provision of enhanced registration aids)

As works got underway in 2014-15, it was also considered prudent to review one further issue:

- Console move (to address the physical remoteness of the organist from the organ, and the resultant acoustic issues, which had existed for 50 years – this element of the works had been seen as "essential" by Martin K Cross)

The tonal improvements to restore brightness to the organ were particularly important when the church was full: At maximum capacity, Aylesford church can hold almost 500 people (as witnessed for the Remembrance Day service in 2014).

MICHAEL J KEAYS

Great pipework 2015, showing the new Mixture III in the foreground

The PCC approved the works on 5/2/2014, and the contract with FH Browne was signed on 18/4/2014 (subject to faculty, which was received on 19/6/2014), for a total of £48,340 excluding VAT; this excluded electrician and transport costs; the console move, approved the following year, added a further £3,790 excluding VAT. Fortunately, the Listed Places of Worship scheme assisted the affordability of the works by allowing the VAT to be reclaimed. The wind supply to the organ had been marginal before the rebuild, and it was thought that a replacement blower might be required; following the rebuild, it would appear that the only likely future costs in this area will be the re-winding of the blower (after over 50 years' service) and some re-leathering of the bellows; a maintenance fund is in place to defray these costs when they arise.

Fundraising

Unlike the 1965 rebuild, when fundraising had barely reached the mid-point by the time works commenced, the funding for the main works in 2015 was already in place prior to the commencement of the rebuild; the 1965 rebuild appears to have assumed some urgency after the initial discussions in 1963, whereas the 2015 rebuild had the benefit of a number of years' discussions, with fundraising running steadily in parallel. When the appeal was re-launched in 2009, after the completion of the toilet / kitchenette, the target for the organ of £50,000 seemed almost impossible: The UK was in the middle of one of the deepest recessions in living memory, and thus finance was tight both corporately and individually; the church had also just finished two major projects (bells restoration and toilet / kitchenette), at a total cost of over £100,000. Encouraging early giving, the vicar launched the appeal on the basis of "it's about £2,000 per year, based on a 25-year expected time until the next works", which made it appear somewhat more achievable. Early on, however, it became clear that external funding bodies, a traditional source of significant income for this type of work, were not in a position to provide much help, so we were in for the long haul.

The level of support for the project, particularly from the vicar, PCC and Congregation was overwhelming: Despite having fund-raised over the previous ten years for the restoration of the bells and the build of a kitchenette and toilet, a large number of initiatives (as detailed in Appendix O) produced the required funding for the organ in advance of the works commencing.

A number of external sponsors also provided useful assistance. In particular, it is interesting to note *(from the vestry meeting minutes of 28/8/1884)* that Aylesford

Supporting the Organ Appeal

Please complete this form and return it to:

The Organ Appeal,
Church Office,
Brassey Centre,
AYLESFORD,
Kent.
ME20 7QR

I would like to contribute: £ [ ]

or Preserve a Pipe from £65, £100 or £130 £ [ ]

or Adopt a Stop £1,000 [ ]

I would like information about leaving a legacy to St Peter & St Paul's Aylesford [ ]

Please make cheques payable to:
Aylesford Parochial Church Council
with "Organ Appeal" written on the back.

Full name ....
Address ....
....
Post Code ....

If you are a **UK Taxpayer** you can increase your gift to us by ticking the following Gift Aid Declaration:

[ ] YES, I would like the Church of St Peter & St Paul in Aylesford to reclaim tax from HMRC on all contributions I make for their work.

I understand that I must pay an amount of income tax at least equal to the amount reclaimed. I am under no obligation to make any further donation and I can cancel this declaration at any time. (If you are unsure if your gift qualifies for Gift Aid tax relief, please ask your local tax office.)

Signature(s) .... Date ....

Proposed specification of the restored Forster & Andrews Organ

Great Organ		Swell Organ	
Open Diapason	8	Tremulant	
Stopt Diapason	8	Open Diapason	8
Dulciana	8	Stopt Diapason	8
Principal	4	Flute d'Amour	8
Nason Flute	4	Principal	4
Twelfth	2⅔	Mixture [E]	III
Fifteenth	2	Cornopean	8
Mixture [N]	III	Oboe	8
Trumpet	8	Trumpet [E]	8

Pedal Organ		Couplers	
Open Diapason	16	Swell to Pedal	
Bourdon	16	Swell to Great	
Octave	8	Swell Octave to Great	
Flute	8	Swell Sub Octave to Great	
Fifteenth	4	Swell Octave	
Flute	4	Swell Sub Octave	
Trumpet [E]	16	Great to Pedal	
Clarion [E]	8		

Thumb and toe pistons
10-level capture system
General cancel

Key: [N] = New; [E] = Extended / Enhanced

St Peter & St Paul's Church, Aylesford, Kent

ORGAN APPEAL

Proposed works and timescale

The work to be undertaken on the organ falls into three main categories:

- CLEANING: Over the years, large amounts of dust and dirt have accumulated, which needs to be removed to assist the reliability of the instrument
- SAFETY: The electrical wiring system dates almost entirely from 1965, and is now in need of replacement with more modern wiring and transmission systems
- TONAL IMPROVEMENTS: The 'sparkle' of the organ has been reduced greatly over the years, mainly as a result of the progressive carpeting of the floors. It is now very difficult to lead a large congregation, and thus these improvements - mainly the restoration of a Mixture stop on the Great manual - are essential

The works also facilitate the moving of the console so that it is closer to the organ itself, a major deficiency since the 1965 rebuild.

The target timescale for the works is early 2012.

How you can help

Any donation that you are able to give will help us to raise the total needed for the works, but you may wish to consider some of the following options as well:

- Preserve a Pipe for £65, £100 or £130
- Adopt a Stop for £1,000
- Support one or more of the many activities advertised in Church in aid of the Organ Appeal
- Make a donation of your choice
- Consider leaving a legacy

Thank you so much for your support.

A brief history of the organ at Aylesford Parish Church

The current organ was built by the Hull firm of Forster and Andrews in 1865, to replace a barrel organ which had stood on the west wall gallery (since removed).

Over the years, the organ has been well maintained, with significant work being undertaken every 25 years or so. In 1965, the organ was moved from the chancel to its current position, electrified, and supplied with a detached console.

Of the 981 pipes which make up the organ today, a large proportion date back to 1865, or to 1879 when Forster and Andrews extended the organ.

The organ is a 2 manual and pedals instrument; it is a good example of Forster and Andrews' work, enhanced visually by casework skilfully painted by a local lady early in the 20th century.

Music at Aylesford Parish Church

Music has been a very important part of Aylesford Parish Church for over 150 years, with the organ continuing to be central to both Sunday worship and to a variety of concerts and other musical events.

The music is directed by the Organist / Choirmaster and his Assistant, who took up their posts in 1985 and 1969 respectively.

Although choir numbers have eased over the last few years, in common with general trends across the country, the choir is still an important part of the church, and is always on the lookout for keen singers of any standard.

Since early 2009, when new facilities were opened in the church, a wider variety of musical activities have been available throughout the year.

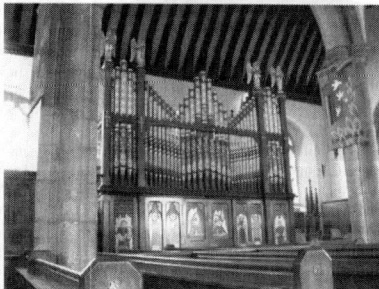

Our vision

We are very fortunate to have a fine Organ in this church, the result of the vision and faith of our Victorian forebears.

In the years since the organ was built, it has been regularly tuned and carefully maintained, and with periodic major work has served the church well for nearly 150 years with very little trouble.

Inevitably, time takes its toll, and it is now time to undertake major work, as described elsewhere on this leaflet, in order to maintain the long-term use of the organ. We are now looking to raise £50,000.

We are aware that we are the current custodians of this fine instrument, and our vision is that the work undertaken will secure the viability of the organ for at least the next 25-50 years, so that future members of the church and Aylesford community will also have the same benefit as we do today.

We hope you will share our vision and commitment to undertake this work, and we trust you will support our Organ Appeal.

The 2015 restoration appeal leaflet

petitioned to the Rochester Bridge Trust for a new bridge at Aylesford, as Aylesford was then contributing funds to the Trust: 130 years later, the Trust contributed funds to Aylesford, making a valuable contribution to the organ appeal!

Periodically, updates were provided in the Parish Magazine, the church website, the weekly "Parish Notes" and on the display boards at the back of church, including a giant thermometer and an organ pipe graphic, both showing overall progress towards the target. There was also a graphic representing each pipe in the organ, coloured-in either where 'sponsored', or 'funded' by general donations, the objective being that all the pipes would be coloured-in once the full £50,000 had been raised. Of course, if this were to be done again, there are now 228 additional pipes, so the re-designed graphic would have to be adapted for use!

FH Browne & Sons, organ builders

FH Browne were established in Deal, Kent, in 1871, by Frederick Henry Browne, an apprentice of William Hobday, a Canterbury organ builder. The business expanded rapidly in the UK, and as far afield as Egypt and Canada. Several of Browne's sons joined the business, which also included the manufacture of pianos, and a music shop selling sheet music, pianos and other instruments. The firm relocated to Canterbury in 1906, under the directorship of William, Frederick Browne's eldest son.

MICHAEL J KEAYS

Steve Bayley, FH Browne & Sons (organ builders) & Sam Walker, 2014

Various members of the Browne family assisted the running of the company after the death of William less than a year after the move to Canterbury, although it was Alfred Willey, an apprentice from before the First World War, who kept the company running right until the end of the Second World War.

The company was then re-formed as FH Browne & Sons (Organ Builders) Ltd, with Alfred Willey (as managing director) and Harry Fagg steadily expanding the company until 1982

when they both died. A new partnership of Roger Greensted (an apprentice since 1963), Reginald Cobb (another employee) and Gordon Chapman (a local organist) was formed, presiding over the move to the Old Cartwright School in Ash (near Canterbury) in 1983. Stephen Bayley bought the company following Roger Greensted's departure in 2013; it is now managed by Steve (as managing director), his wife, Yvette and (since April 2015) the author. A number of the current employees were formerly with Manders, including Steve Bayley, Les Ross (works manager until retirement in 2015), and Matt Fry.

With over 600 organs in their care, FH Browne's clients are spread across the UK, and as far afield as the Falkland Islands.

2015 – The Forster & Andrews organ's 150th anniversary

Refurbishment and expansion

Work commenced on the dismantling of the organ on Monday 15/9/2014. Pipework for revoicing was returned to Browne's workshops, together with the console (for rewiring and modernisation). Reassembly on site was managed by Matt Fry, of FH Browne.

In addition to complete rewiring and cleaning, and providing a mobile platform for the console, the major works on the organ comprised tonal alterations and console modernisation.

The scope of the tonal alterations was the addition of the bottom octave of the Swell Mixture III, reinstatement of a Great Mixture III, and the extension of the Trumpet 8' to provide a Pedal Trombone 16' and Great Clarion 4'.

The console modernisation included the refurbishment of the manuals and pedalboard, additional tabs for the new stops, a tab to enable the Great reeds to be played on the Swell, six combination pistons to each division and six 'Generals' (operating across the entire organ), a new 'General Cancel' thumb piston, and a reversible Pedal Reed toe piston. Pistons were provided both in the key slips (thumb pistons) and in the pedal sweep (toe pistons). A 'Setter' thumb piston enabled the setting of each of the combination pistons in any one of ten player-selected ways. A new transmission and control system between the console and organ was provided using Solid State Logic, a system of switching for pipe organs which was established in 1969 and is now installed in thousands of organs throughout the world. An indicator light was installed on the console, to be operated remotely from the west end of the church to announce, for example, the arrival of brides.

For a few weeks after the commencement of works, an electronic organ was provided as a temporary instrument; from November 2014, and for the remainder of the works, FH Browne provided a one manual and pedals "Cantuar" organ, which they had built in 1957. Whilst reassembling the organ, the correct positioning of the casework panels (as shown in photographs from the early 20th century) was re-established: The organ is now visually cohesive once again, with the undecorated pipework and panels together on the east side of the organ.

The organ restoration was completed on Thursday 25/6/2015, with the re-opening service being on Sunday 28/6/2015. For this, the "Huit invocations pour orgue", written in 2011 by Denis Bédard, was used to bring the main organ back into its central role in the support of the worship at Aylesford. The voluntary was Widor's "Toccata" from the 5th organ symphony.

The organ weekend of 14th – 15th November 2015 included the opening recital by David Newsholme, assistant organist at Canterbury Cathedral on the Sunday afternoon, preceded by a talk and recital by the author, entitled "Discover the Organ", on the Saturday. One of the pieces played on the Saturday was a newly composed piece by the author, "Jubilee Jubilate", which showcased the changes in the organ's 150th anniversary year, as well as Frederic Wood's 'Aylesford Bridge'.

The specification of the organ following the 2015 rebuild, including the Mixtures compositions, can be seen on the next pages.

Opening Organ Recital
on the newly rebuilt
1865 Forster & Andrews organ
at
St Peter & St Paul's Church, Aylesford

DAVID NEWSHOLME

Assistant Organist of
Canterbury Cathedral

Sunday, 15th November 2015
3.00pm
Tickets: £9 (including refreshments)
In advance from the church office (01622 719366)
or Michael (01622 719589), or on the door

Poster for the 2015 opening recital

2015 SPECIFICATION
FH Browne & Sons Ltd

Compass: Manuals CC - g3, 56 note.
Pedals CCC - F, 30 note.
Electric Action, solid state transmission 3" wind.
Pitch: A=445.3 Hz

Great

1.	Open Diapason *	8'
2.	Stopt Diapason *	8'
3.	Dulciana *	8'
4.	Principal *	4'
5.	Nason Flute	4'
6.	Twelfth *	2 2/3'
7.	Fifteenth *	2'
8.	Mixture	III
9.	Trumpet	8'
10.	Clarion	4'

Pedal
(RCO, Willis pattern)

18.	Open Diapason **	16'
19.	Bourdon *	16'
20.	Principal ++	8'
21.	Flute +	8'
22.	Fifteenth ++	4'
23.	Flute +	4'
24.	Trombone	16'
25.	Trumpet	8'

Swell (enclosed)

11.	Open Diapason +	8'
12.	Stopt Diapason *	8'
13.	Flûte d'Amour +	8'
	(TC, CC-BB from No 10)	
14.	Principal *	4'
15.	Mixture	III
16.	Cornopean +	8'
17.	Oboe +	8'

Mixture compositions
Great
1-12 - 19.22.26
13-24 - 15.19.22
25-48 - 12.15.19
49-56 - 8.12.15
Swell
1-31 - 15.19.22
32-49 - 12.15.19
50-56 - 8.12.15

Solid State Logic transmission
& control

Notes:
Ranks wholly or partially original have been indicated in the specification, by way of reference.
F&A 1865 pipework: Wholly [*]; partially [+].
F&A 1879 pipework: Wholly [**]; partially [++].

2015 SPECIFICATION
FH Browne & Sons Ltd

Continued from page 121

Accessories

26. Swell to Great
27. Swell Oct. to Great
28. Swell Sub Oct to Gt.
29. Swell to Pedal
30. Great to Pedal
31. Gt & Ped pistons coupled
32. Swell Octave
33. Swell Sub Octave
34. Great Reeds on Swell
35. Swell Tremulant
36. Balanced Swell pedal
37. 6 adjustable combination thumb pistons to each manual
38. 6 adjustable General combination thumb pistons
39. 6 adjustable Pedal combination toe pistons
40. 6 adjustable Gen / Sw combination toe pistons (switchable)
41. 3 reversible pistons for 26, 29 & 30
42. 3 reversible toe pistons for 24, 26 & 30
43. General Cancel
44. Setter
45. 10 levels of memory with channel lock & channel locked indicator West End indicator light central on console tab rail Double-touch tab stops with switchable divisional cancel

(1240 pipes)

Notes:
8 new.
9 extended 12 notes in each of treble & bass, to form Great 4' Clarion & Pedal.
16' Trombone; placed on off-note chests.
15 completed (new bottom octave).
10, 24 & 25 from 9.
18 & 20 reverted to original names .
20 & 22 from 18.
21 & 23 from 19.
37, 38, 39 & 40 new.
42, 43, 44 & 45 new.
41. Reversible 29 new.
Detached console, Mander, restored & modified FH Browne.
Console relocated on new mobile plinth (generally positioned behind choir stalls).

The programme for the opening recital contained the following pieces:
JS Bach *Prelude and Fugue in C* (BWV 545); JS Bach *Liebster Jesu, wir sind hier* (BWV 731); WA Mozart *Fantasia in F Minor* (K 608); Percy Whitlock *Five Short Pieces*; CM Widor *Allegro from Symphony 6* (Op.42, no.2); Noel Rawsthorne *Prelude on the Londonderry Air*; Edward Elgar arr. George Martin *Imperial March*; Edward Elgar *Salut d'amour*; CM Widor *Finale from Symphony 6* (Op.42, no.2).

A series of recitals by visiting organists will continue from 2016, potentially sponsored by a local company. Recitalists who have agreed to perform include:

David Flood (Canterbury Cathedral); Paul Hale (Southwell Minster); Paul Isom (St Luke's Sevenoaks); Joe Sentance (St Stephen's Walbrook, City of London); Nigel Groome (St George's Beckenham); Roger Sayer (Temple Church, London); David Poulter (Liverpool Cathedral)

It is also planned to use the rebuilt organ to encourage younger players, potentially through the use of a scholarship scheme.

The location of the console

Whilst the organ was originally built with an integrated console (using tracker rods to control the organ action), a detached console, electrically connected to the organ, was provided as part of the 1965 works. At this point, the organ moved to the north nave aisle, but the console was placed in the Lady Chapel, immediately behind the choir. With the permanent move of the choir to the nave in 1978, consideration was also given to moving the console, as shown in plans drawn-up at the time by Roy Burgess. The identified position was on the south wall, behind the choir and in front of the pulpit – a position which was again considered as an option in 2015. On 8/8/1978, Rev Alec T Goodrich wrote to Manders asking their opinion. The move was seen as impractical, most likely due to the difficulties of extending the wiring loom connecting the console and organ, and so the console remained in the Lady Chapel.

The initial scope of the 1987 works also looked at moving the console, to the north aisle position behind the choir, and Manders quoted for this: Although this work was not carried out in 1987, the opportunity arose again during the 2015 works and after considering various positions, agreement was reached (and supported by the Parochial Church Council (PCC) and Diocesan Organ Advisor (DOA) in February

2015) to move the console to the north aisle position, on a mobile plinth, enabling it to be moved out of the way to accommodate bands and orchestras in the space when required, and to move it into the nave for recitals.

The console relocation was finally achieved, some 37 years after the original plans had been made; FH Browne constructed the mobile plinth and moved the console onto it in parallel with the 2015 organ restoration works.

The future: 2015 onwards

The Forster and Andrews organ at Aylesford, modest in comparison to some pipe organs, is nevertheless a good and very flexible instrument. The music of Aylesford church has been a key factor in bringing people into the church family for over a century and a half; with the organ and console refurbished, and the console in a flexible position, Aylesford is now positioned once again to attract people into the church with the music, as performers (recitalists or organ scholars), as members of the choir, or as appreciative members of the congregation whose worship can be lifted by the legacy first bequeathed to Aylesford church by our distant Victorian benefactors.

The history of Aylesford organ does not stop here: Over the coming years, minor works and cleanings will be required – that is the nature of a mechanical device in regular use – and for this reason a maintenance fund has been set-up to help defray future expenses. At some point, the blower will need re-winding (last done 50 years ago), and the bellows re-leathering (last done possibly even longer ago). There will be more interesting and amusing anecdotes around the organ, the organists and the choir – and it is these that provide the rich tapestry of the history of any place. We have been given a great legacy and, as the appeal leaflet for the 2015 restoration stated, "We are aware that we are the current custodians of this fine instrument, and our vision is that the work undertaken will secure the viability of the organ … so that future members of the church and Aylesford community will also have the same benefit as we do today."

If nothing else, this book has uncovered and consolidated the deep and rich history of the music of the parish, and the dedication and commitment of so many, right up to the present day. The church in Aylesford owes a huge debt of gratitude to our forebears, and bears a great responsibility for the future. The past should continue to be our inspiration, the present our opportunity, and the future our duty to safeguard.

A final thought

Built just two years after the opening of what is now the London Underground, and in the same year that the Salvation Army was formed, the Forster & Andrews organ at Aylesford Parish Church is now 150 years old and has reached a fine maturity of tone. Whilst the organ has developed over the years, to meet changing needs and emerging technology (action electrification in 1965, computerised transmission control in 2015), a large part of the organ (particularly the pipework and some of the action) is original. It continues to provide essential support in worship and in the life and mission of the church in Aylesford. A typical Forster & Andrews organ, it is very solidly constructed, and has stood the test of time for a century and a half already: Provided it is well looked after, both in terms of regular maintenance and stable atmospheric conditions, there is even reason to believe (and this is a view upheld by the current maintainers of the instrument) that the organ should be perfectly usable for another three or four hundred years. There has been a great revival in the sphere of pipe organs over the last quarter of a century, with the realisation that although an expensive electronic organ can now imitate a pipe organ quite effectively, it cannot provide the same tonal impact, or 'punch', that a pipe organ is able to and, more significantly, it will never come anywhere near the potential lifespan of a pipe organ, which could easily be in the order of half a millennium (as demonstrated by surviving instruments, mainly on the European mainland). Whilst the cost of keeping a pipe organ in service is expensive, it is a far better long-term investment, both economically and musically, than an electronic equivalent; it speaks too of the commitment and dedication of the community, and to the worship of God, over very many generations.

In a quiet moment, try to think of the Aylesford instrument historically, "one of the finest parish church organs in the county" *(Kent Messenger, 1965)* – all the services it has accompanied, the weddings, the funerals, the occasions joyful and sad: It has been the vehicle of worship for many generations of people in this church, and it will continue to be so for many generations to come.

"Loud organs, his glory forth tell in deep tone"

(H W Baker, 1821-1877)

Appendices

Appendices Summary

Appendix A

Aylesford parish church changes since 1837 – Overview summary timeline

1837	First organist appointed (John Wagon)
1838	Gallery built; barrel organ purchased
1840	Organ in Aylesford Vicarage
1840s	(mid to late). Emigration from Aylesford to Australia
1851	New vestry built on north side of the church; window on west end of north wall blocked-in
1852	Renovation of the church
1862	Removal of organ from Aylesford Vicarage
1863	Harmonium starts to be used for services
1865	New Forster & Andrews organ installed in the gallery; barrel organ removed
1866	Aylesford Church Choir formed (boys and men), sometime between January and Easter (1/4/1866)
1868-9	Alterations to the chancel
1878-9	Dismantling of the gallery and restoration of the church
1879	Move of organ to the North Aisle Chancel (Lady Chapel); windows blocked-up; organ expanded significantly (casework increases in size); angels placed on top of casework pillars; decoration of the case pipework
c.1890-1907	Decoration of the organ casework
1892	Unveiling of the Brassey Memorial window
1894	Further works on the organ
1908	New vestry built (extension of the 1851 vestry); old vestry door blocked-up; organ cleaned
1947	Trumpet stop added to organ. Pulpit moved to the south aisle? Ladies join choir on a temporary basis
1950	Ladies admitted to the choir on a permanent basis
1965	Organ moved to the north aisle, enlarged, electrified and provided with a detached console in the Lady Chapel

1966	Lady Chapel windows restored
1977-78	Choir moved from chancel to nave
1987	Organ cleaned & overhauled
2006	Bells restoration
2008	Kitchenette and toilet facilities provided; font moved forwards from under the tower
2015	Organ restoration, modernisation and enlargement (including Pedal Trombone stop and restoration of the Great Mixture); console moved to north aisle, behind choir stalls

Appendix B

List of organs built or altered by Forster & Andrews (Hull) in Kent
From ledger and order books

Extracted from National Archives listing (held by Hull History Centre), with cross-referencing to, and updates from, National Pipe Organ Register (NPOR, www.npor.org.uk). *Note: This list may be incomplete - many of F&A's records were lost in 1941*

Location	Date	Order	Page	Ledger	Notes
Addington					
St Margaret	**1883**	885	49	O6	
	1906		180	O9	
Aylesford					
St Peter	**1865**		338	LC	
	1865	375	102	O2	*Corrected (incorrectly listed as Entry 275). Refers to Ledger 338*
	1879	375	98	O5	*Repairs & Additions: Feb. 1879*
	1879	375	99	O5	*Repairs & Additions: Nov. 1879*
	1894	15	65	O8	*Order number is misleading*
	1908		38	O10	
Beckenham					
St George	**1887**	979	32	O7	
	1897		151	O8	
	1905		169	O9	
	1911	979	83	O10	
Wesleyan	**1887**	999	41	O7	
	1907		12	O10	
Birling					
Christ Church	**1906**				*Only on NPOR. Lower Birling (now part of Snodland)*
Blackheath					
Wesleyan	**1915**		173	O10	
Bromley					
Baptist	**1885**	952	133	O6	
Christ Church	**1887**		37	O7	
Wesleyan	**1889**		109	O7	
	1901		88	O9	
	1915		174	O10	

Location	Date	Order	Page	Ledger	Notes
Canterbury					
Baptist	**1890**	1058	127	O7	
Congregational	**1914**	1368	152	O10	
	1885	939	117	O6	
	1899		33	O9	
St Paul	**1900**	1261	53	O9	
	1906		6	O10	
	<undated>		65	O9	
Chatham					
St Paul	**1892**	1110	11	O8	*Technically, "St Paul with All Saints"*
	1897		154	O8	
	1906		182	O9	
	1912		108	O10	
	1914		150	O10	
Cheriton					
All Souls	**1897**	1202	150	O8	
Chislehurst					
Je Vanner	**1890**	912	146	O7	*Private organ for the Vanner family, Beechcroft House*
Wesleyan	**1870**	487	70	O3	
	1873	487	69	O4	*Addition to 1870 organ? NPOR has this as St Nicholas*
	1883	884	48	O6	*Addition to 1870 organ? NPOR has this as St Nicholas (& 1884?)*
	1901		72	O9	
Cranbrook					
School	**1860s**				*Only on NPOR. 2nd hand from elsewhere*
Crayford					
St Paulinus	**1879**				*Only on NPOR*
Cuxton					
St Michael & All Angels	**1881**	854	10	O6	
	1908		47	O10	
Farnborough					
St Giles the Abbot	**1889**				*Only on NPOR*
Farningham					
St Peter & St Paul	**1879**				*Only on NPOR*
Frindsbury					
All Saints	**1889**	1053	117	O7	

Location	Date	Order	Page	Ledger	Notes
Great Chart					
St Mary's	1854		149	LA	
Harbledown					
St Michael & All Angels	1882	848	1	O6	*St Michael's history cites a date of 1879*
Herne Bay					
Christ Church	1880				*Only on NPOR*
Horsmonden					
St Margaret	1896		13	O7	
Kemsing					
St Mary the Virgin	1877	742	37	O5	
Lee					
St Augustine's, Grove Park	1888	104	62	O7	
	1892				*Only on NPOR*
	1901				*Only on NPOR*
St Peter	1887		27	O7	*The church is now in a new building*
Lewisham					
Wesleyan	1889		114	O7	
Leybourne					
Catholic	1904	1315	141	O9	
St Peter & St Paul	1888	1028	84	O7	
Luton (Chatham)					
Christ Church	1892				*Only on NPOR.* *Assumed alterations / additions only*
Maidstone					
Lord Romney	<undated>		75	O1	*Private organ, in Mote House*
St John	1860		239	LB	*Mote Park (seat of the Earl of Romney)* *Church opened 1861*
	1866		124	O2	
New Brompton					
St Marks	1885	956	137	O6	*Now St Mark, Gillingham*
	1913		143	O10	
Plumstead Common					
Wesleyan	1871	521	109	O3	
Rainham					
St Margaret	1880				*Only on NPOR*

Location	Date	Order	Page	Ledger	Notes
Ramsgate					
Congregational	**1893**	1127	33	O8	
	1906		7	O10	
	1911		102	O10	
Rochester					
Bethel Chapel	**1876**	705	163	O4	
Cathedral	**1876**		12	O5	*New pipework for the case*
St Batholomew's Hospital	**1872**	569	20	O4	*'Hospital' added (per NPOR)*
St Margaret	**1880**	824	134	O5	*St Margaret's history cites a date of 1877*
Wesleyan	**1905**		160	O9	
Seal					
Congregational	**1881**	832	144	O5	
St Peter & St Paul	**1878**	786	84-85	O5	
	1915		172	O10	
Sevenoaks					
St John the Baptist	**1889**	1038	96	O7	
St Nicholas	**1896**	1178	115-116	O8	
Sidcup					
Congregational	**1881**	832	144	O5	
Tunbridge Wells					
Congregational (Albion Rd?)	**1895**	337	88	O8	
Congregational Mount Pleasant	**1885**	941	119	O6	
Wickhambreaux					
St Andrew	**1879**	734	111	O5	
	1902		117	O9	
Wingham					
St Mary the Virgin	**1886**	970	156	O6	
Woolwich					
Congregational Rectory Place	**1882**	855	11	O6	
	1923		241	O10	
Wrotham					
St George	**1883**	894	60	O6	
	1899		26	O9	

Ref.	Ledger / Order Book	Period Covered
LA	Forster/1/LA	1844-1857
LB	Forster/1/LB	1857-1864
LC	Forster/1/LC	1864-1866
O1	Forster/1/O1	1853-1866
O2	Forster/1/O2	1851-1867
O3	Forster/1/O3	1867-1872
O4	Forster/1/O4	1872-1876

Ref.	Ledger / Order Book	Period Covered
O5	Forster/1/O5	1876-1881
O6	Forster/1/O6	1881-1886
O7	Forster/1/O7	1886-1891
O8	Forster/1/O8	1892-1899
O9	Forster/1/O9	1898-1906
O10	Forster/1/O10	1906-1925

Forster & Andrews organs: Chronological listing of work in Kent
(New or alterations / additions)

Note: This list is incomplete – many of F&A's records were lost in 1941

Location	Church	Year
Great Chart	St Mary	1854
Maidstone	St John	1860
Aylesford	St Peter	1865
Maidstone	St John	1866
Cranbrook	School	1860s
Chislehurst	Wesleyan	1870
Plumstead Common	Wesleyan	1871
Rochester	St Batholomew's Hospital	1872
Chislehurst	Wesleyan	1873
Rochester	Bethel Chapel	1876
Rochester	Cathedral	1876
Kemsing	St Mary the Virgin	1877
Seal	St Peter & St Paul	1878
Aylesford	St Peter	1879 (Feb)
Aylesford	St Peter	1879 (Nov)
Crayford	St Paulinus	1879
Farningham	St Peter & St Paul	1879
Wickhambreaux	St Andrew	1879
Herne Bay	Christ Church	1880
Rainham	St Margaret	1880

Location	Church	Year
Rochester	St Margaret	1880
Cuxton	St Michael & All Angels	1881
Seal	Congregational	1881
Sidcup	Congregational	1881
Harbledown	St Michael & All Angels	1882
Woolwich	Congregational	1882
Addington	St Margaret	1883
Chislehurst	Wesleyan	1883
Wrotham	St George	1883
Bromley	Baptist	1885
Canterbury	Congregational, Guildhall St	1885
New Brompton	St Mark	1885
Tunbridge Wells	Congregational, Mount Pleasant	1885
Wingham	St Mary the Virgin	1886
Beckenham	St George	1887
Beckenham	Wesleyan	1887
Bromley	Christ Church	1887
Lee	St Peter	1887
Lee, Grove Park	St Augustine	1888
Leybourne	St Peter & St Paul	1888
Bromley	Wesleyan	1889
Farnborough	St Giles the Abbot	1889
Frindsbury	All Saints	1889
Lewisham	Wesleyan	1889
Sevenoaks	St John the Baptist	1889
Canterbury	Baptist	1890
Chislehurst	Je Vanner (residence)	1890
Chatham	St Paul	1892
Lee, Grove Park	St Augustine	1892
Luton (Chatham)	Christ Church	1892
Ramsgate	Congregational	1893
Aylesford	St Peter	1894
Tunbridge Wells	Congregational	1895
Horsmonden	St Margaret	1896
Sevenoaks	St Nicholas	1896
Beckenham	St George	1897
Chatham	St Paul	1897

Location	Church	Year
Cheriton	All Souls	1897
Canterbury	Congregational, Guildhall St	1899
Wrotham	St George	1899
Canterbury	St Paul	1900
Bromley	Wesleyan	1901
Chislehurst	Wesleyan	1901
Lee, Grove Park	St Augustine	1901
Wickhambreaux	St Andrew	1902
Leybourne	Catholic	1904
Beckenham	St George	1905
Rochester	Wesleyan	1905
Addington	St Margaret	1906
Birling	Christ Church	1906
Canterbury	St Paul	1906
Chatham	St Paul	1906
Ramsgate	Congregational	1906
Beckenham	Wesleyan	1907
Aylesford	St Peter	1908
Cuxton	St Michael & All Angels	1908
Beckenham	St George	1911
Ramsgate	Congregational Hall	1911
Chatham	St Paul	1912
New Brompton	St Mark	1913
Canterbury	Congregational	1914
Chatham	St Paul	1914
Blackheath	Wesleyan	1915
Bromley	Wesleyan	1915
Seal	St Peter	1915
Woolwich	Rectory Place Congregational	1923
Canterbury	St Paul	<undated>
Maidstone	Lord Romney (residence)	<undated>

Forster & Andrews organs in Kent:
Estimate of new organs / additions

(NB: Not always clear from records listing which is which)
Note: This list is incomplete – many of F&A's records were lost in 1941

Location	New	Additions	Notes
Addington	1	1	
Aylesford	1	4	
Beckenham	2	4	
Birling	1		
Blackheath		1	*Assumed addition only*
Bromley	3	2	
Canterbury	3	4	
Chatham	1	4	
Cheriton	1		
Chislehurst	2	3	
Crayford	1		
Cuxton	1	1	
Farnborough	1		
Farningham	1		
Frindsbury	1		
Great Chart	1		
Harbledown	1		
Herne Bay	1		
Horsmonden	1		
Kemsing	1		
Lee	1	3	*St Peter's assumed addition only*
Lewisham	1		*Assumed addition only*
Leybourne	2		
Luton (Chatham)		1	*Assumed addition only*
Maidstone	2	1	
New Brompton	1	1	*Now part of Gillingham*
Plumstead Common	1		
Rainham	1		
Ramsgate	1	2	
Rochester	3	2	

Location	New	Additions	Notes
Seal	2	1	
Sevenoaks	2		*Both assumed new*
Sidcup	1		
Tunbridge Wells	2		*Assumed two different churches, and both assumed new*
Wickhambreaux	1	1	
Wingham	1		
Woolwich	1	1	
Wrotham	1	1	
TOTAL:	**48**	**39**	

Appendix D

Layout of the organ at St Peter & St Paul's Church, Aylesford

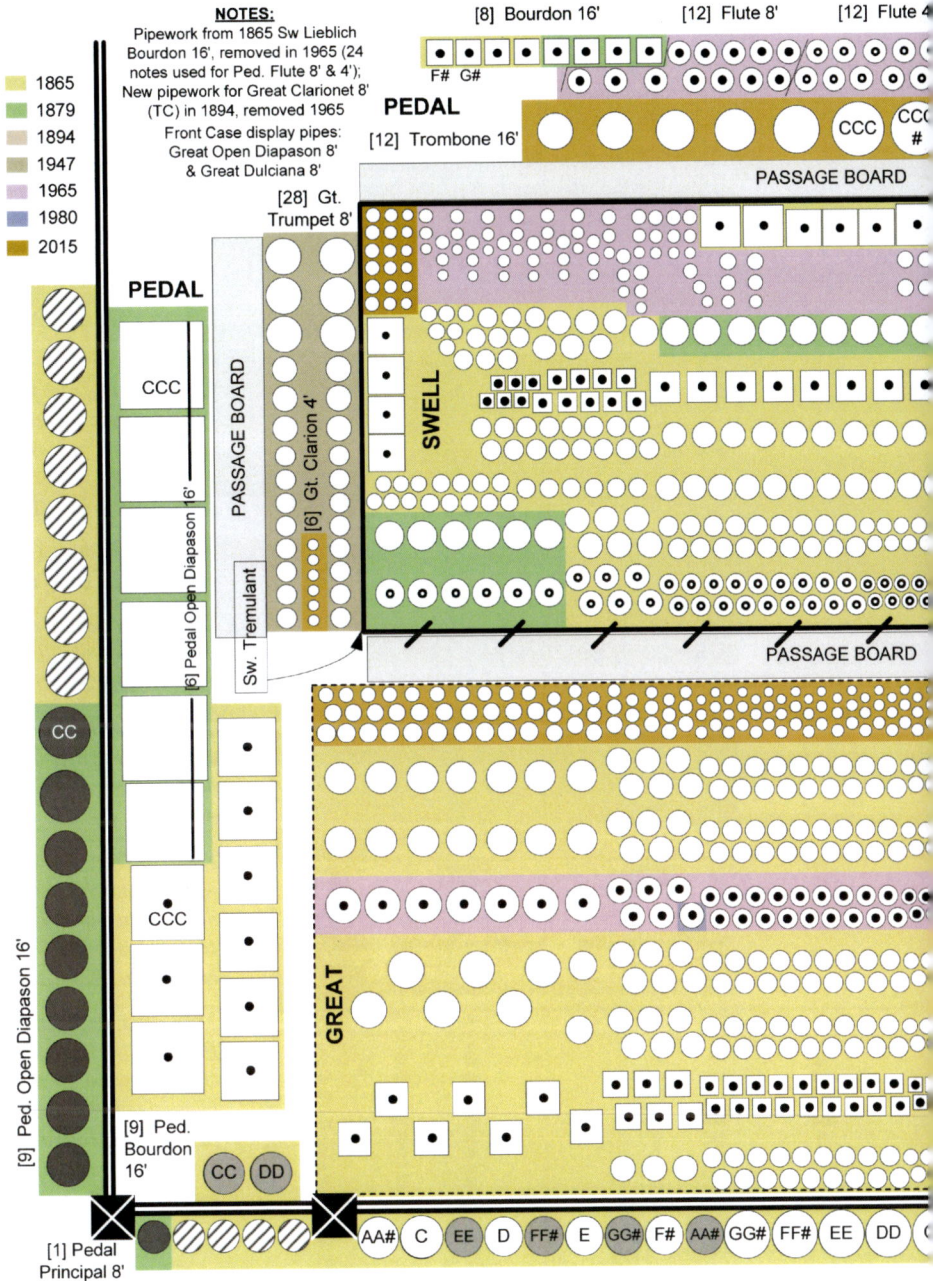

NOTES:
Pipework from 1865 Sw Lieblich Bourdon 16', removed in 1965 (24 notes used for Ped. Flute 8' & 4'); New pipework for Great Clarionet 8' (TC) in 1894, removed 1965

Front Case display pipes: Great Open Diapason 8' & Great Dulciana 8'

Legend:
- 1865
- 1879
- 1894
- 1947
- 1965
- 1980
- 2015

[8] Bourdon 16'   [12] Flute 8'   [12] Flute 4'

F# G#

PEDAL

[12] Trombone 16'

CCC   CCC#

PASSAGE BOARD

[28] Gt. Trumpet 8'

PEDAL

CCC

[6] Pedal Open Diapason 16'

PASSAGE BOARD

Sw. Tremulant

[6] Gt. Clarion 4'

SWELL

PASSAGE BOARD

CCC

CC

[9] Ped. Open Diapason 16'

GREAT

[9] Ped. Bourdon 16'

CC   DD

[1] Pedal Principal 8'

AA#   C   EE   D   FF#   E   GG#   F#   AA#   GG#   FF#   EE   DD

The following time chart tracks the development of the organ over its first 150 years.

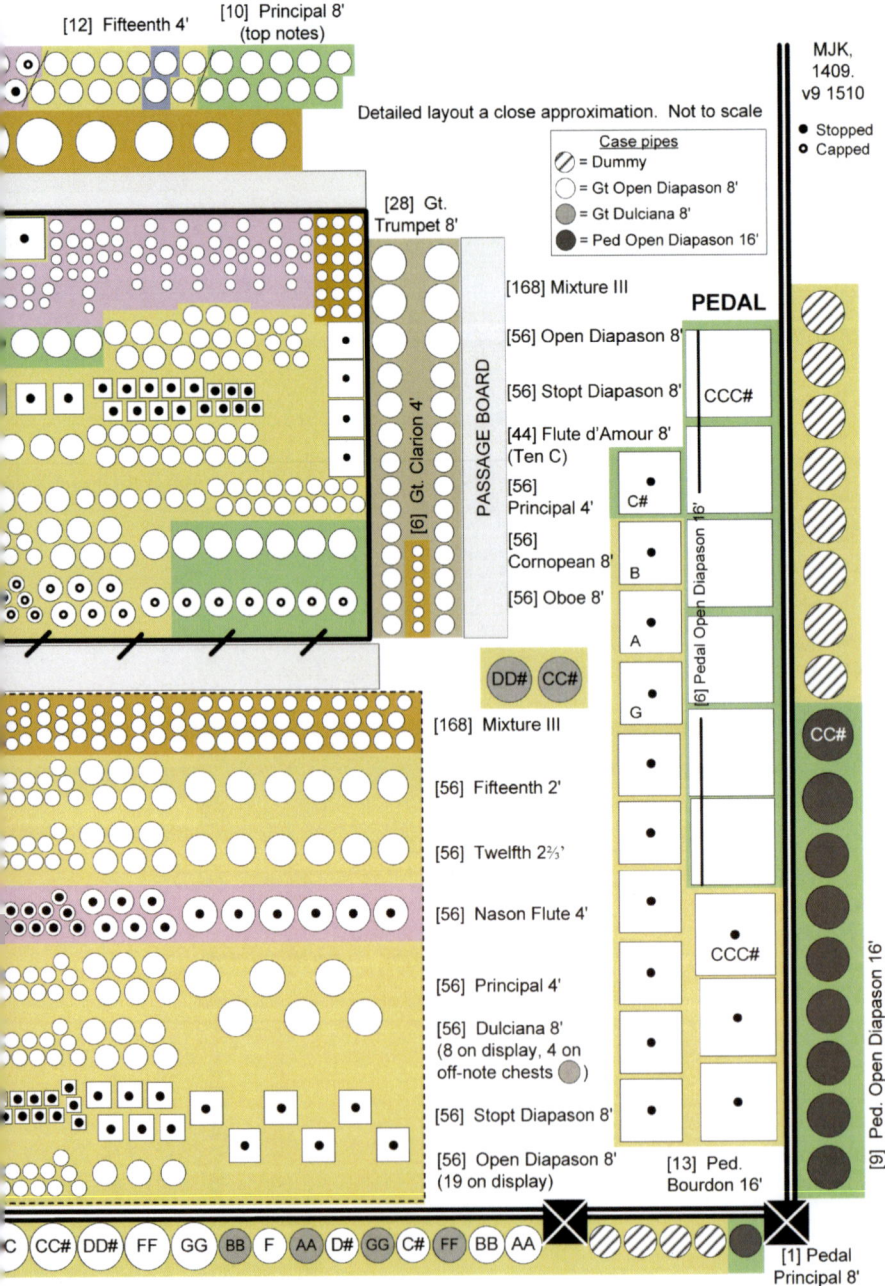

[12] Fifteenth 4'

[10] Principal 8' (top notes)

MJK, 1409. v9 1510

Detailed layout a close approximation. Not to scale

Case pipes
⊘ = Dummy
○ = Gt Open Diapason 8'
● = Gt Dulciana 8'
● = Ped Open Diapason 16'

● Stopped
○ Capped

[28] Gt. Trumpet 8'

PEDAL

[168] Mixture III

[56] Open Diapason 8'

[56] Stopt Diapason 8'

CCC#

[44] Flute d'Amour 8' (Ten C)

PASSAGE BOARD

[56] Principal 4'

C#

[56] Cornopean 8'

B

[6] Gt. Clarion 4'

[56] Oboe 8'

A

G

DD# CC#

[168] Mixture III

[56] Fifteenth 2'

[56] Twelfth 2⅔'

[56] Nason Flute 4'

[6] Pedal Open Diapason 16'

CC#

[56] Principal 4'

CCC#

[56] Dulciana 8' (8 on display, 4 on off-note chests ●)

[56] Stopt Diapason 8'

[56] Open Diapason 8' (19 on display)

[13] Ped. Bourdon 16'

[9] Ped. Open Diapason 16'

C CC# DD# FF GG BB F AA D# GG C# FF BB AA

[1] Pedal Principal 8'

Appendix E

Aylesford organ pipework age analysis

The time chart below indicates the age and evolution of all the pipework in the Aylesford organ.

Year	Added	Removed	Total
	Great		
1865	560	0	560
1879	0	0	560
1894	44	168	438
1947	56	0	492
1965	56	100	448
1980	1	1	448
2015	180	0	628

Year	Added	Removed	Total
	Pedal		
1865	25	0	25
1879	47	0	72
1894	0	0	72
1947	0	0	72
1965	36 *	0	108
1980	2	2	108
2015	12	0	120

	Swell		
1865	332	0	332
1879	48	0	380
1894	0	0	380
1947	0	0	380
1965	132	56	456
1980	0	0	456
2015	36	0	492

	Total Speaking Pipes		
1865	917	0	917
1879	95	0	1012
1894	44	168	888
1947	56	0	944
1965	224 *	156	1012
1980	3	3	1012
2015	228	0	1240

Year	Added	Removed	Total
	Total Dummy Pipes		
1865	34	0	34
1879	0	10	24
1894	0	0	24
1947	0	0	24
1965	0	0	24
1980	0	0	24
2015	0	0	24

* 12 reused from 1865 (Swell Lieblich Bourdon 16')

Age of current pipework

Year of origin	Great	Swell	Pedal	Speaking Pipes		Dummy
				Total	%	
1865	336	288	37	661	53.31%	24
1879	0	36	47	83	6.69%	0
1894	0	0	0	0	0.00%	0
1947	56	0	0	56	4.52%	0
1965	55	132	22	209	16.85%	0
1980	1	0	2	3	0.24%	0
2015	180	36	12	228	18.39%	0
Totals	**628**	**492**	**120**	**1240**	**100.00%**	**24**

Speaking pipework

New pipework was provided for the Great Clarionet 8' (44 pipes, to Tenor C) in 1894, but this rank was fully removed in 1965.

Three pipes were replaced in 1980 (one from the Great Nason Flute 4' and two from the Pedal Fifteenth 4'), after the originals had gone missing.

The current Pedal fluework (i.e. excluding the 12 pipes for the Pedal Trombone 16') includes 12 pipes from the discarded 1865 Swell Lieblich Bourdon 16', revoiced as Pedal Fifteenth 4' extension, the remaining 44 of the 56 Swell Lieblich Bourdon pipes were discarded. The age of the current Pedal fluework (i.e. excluding the Pedal reed), is as follows:

Date	Stop	No. of pipes	Notes
1865	Pedal Bourdon 16'	25	
	Swell Lieblich Bourdon 16'	12	*Reused as Pedal extension in 1965: Fifteenth 4'. Two of these were replaced in 1980*
	Total	**37**	
1879	Pedal Open Diapason 16'	25	
	Pedal Open Diapason 16'	5	*Pedalboard extension*
	Pedal Bourdon 16'	5	*Pedalboard extension*
	Pedal Open Diapason 16'	12	*Pedal extension: Pedal Principal 8'*
	Total	**47**	
1965	Pedal Open Diapason 16'	24	*Pedal extensions: Pedal Flute 8' & 4'*
	Total	**24**	
	Grand total	**108**	*(i.e. two ranks of 54 notes (30+12+12))*

Dummy pipes

In 1865, the organ had non-speaking dummy pipes on both sides; all front case pipework comprised speaking pipes (a mixture of Great Open Diapason 8' and Great Dulciana 8').

Ten dummy pipes were discarded in November 1879, as part of the extension of the organ; eight other dummy pipes (four from each side) were moved to the front of the case, adjacent to the central pillars in the newly-created 'wings'; 18 pipes of the Pedal Open Diapason 16' filled the 18 positions vacated in the disposal or moving of the dummy pipes. Two pipes of the Pedal Principal 8' were positioned at the far ends of the front of the case.

Appendix F

Aylesford organists & assistant organists

Organists		Assistant Organists	
Barrel organ			
John Wagon	1838 - 1864		
Silas Wagon	1865 - 1865?		
F&A organ			
John Humphreys	1866 - 1879 (Nov?)		
Harold Woolley	1879 - 1890 (Nov?)		
John (Jack) Walmsley	1890 - c.1895 *	H Burgiss-Brown +	early 1890s
Charles F Manglesdorff	c.1895 - 1902	Eric Dine +	c.1902
Agnes Thorndike	1902 - 1909		
William (Billy) Wilson	1909 - 1946 * (Jun)	Mrs Everett +	c.1915 - 1941?
Harold Moore	1946 - 1969 (Jun)	Gary Tollerfield Roy Lampard (Organist of St Mark's, Eccles)	1962 - 1967 1967? - 1968
Peter Dawson	1970 - 1974	**HELEN TURNER**	1968 - present (Jan)
Roy Burgess	1975 - 1985 (Feb)	John Brown + Alan McCrerie + (Organist of Aylesford Methodist Church)	1980s 1990s
MICHAEL J KEAYS	1985 - present (Sept)	Christopher Haydon +	1998 - 2004

The longest tenure of the organist at Aylesford is currently (2015) Billy Wilson (37 years as organist, then assisted for at least a further five years).

The longest tenure of the assistant organist at Aylesford is currently (2015) Helen Turner (47 years).

Notes:
Current organist & assistant organist shown in **BOLD** *type.*
John Wagon appointed 25th March 1837.
Organists were also choirmaster (except for Agnes Thorndike, when Rev Arthur Thorndike, her husband and the vicar, was choirmaster).
* Jack Walmsley resumed the post of organist & choirmaster late in the First World War, until Billy Wilson returned (early 1919).
+ Assisted occasionally.
Billy Wilson continued to assist occasionally after he had resigned the organist position, until the early 1950s. Harold Moore continued to assist for a few months after he had resigned the organist position in 1969, until his death in November 1970.
Agnes Thorndike & Mrs Everett were both vicar's wives.
Eric Dine was headmaster at the boys' school.

Appendix G

Aylesford vicars since 1832

This list has been compiled from the board on the north wall of the church, with minor corrections from research (including wills detailed by an unknown person, held at Kent History & Library Centre, Maidstone, and the UK Clergy List 1897).

1832	William Staines
1840	Edward Marsh
1862	Anthony Grant
1878	Cyril Grant (son of Anthony Grant)
1895	George Vaux
1902	Arthur Thorndike
1909	Thomas Sopwith
1915	Frederick Everett
1941	Trevor Southgate
1950	Henry Powell
1964	Alec T Goodrich
1980	Arthur Heathcote
1990	Paul Francis
2000	Simon Tillotson
2007	Christopher van Straaten

Appendix H

The family of Edward Garrard Marsh

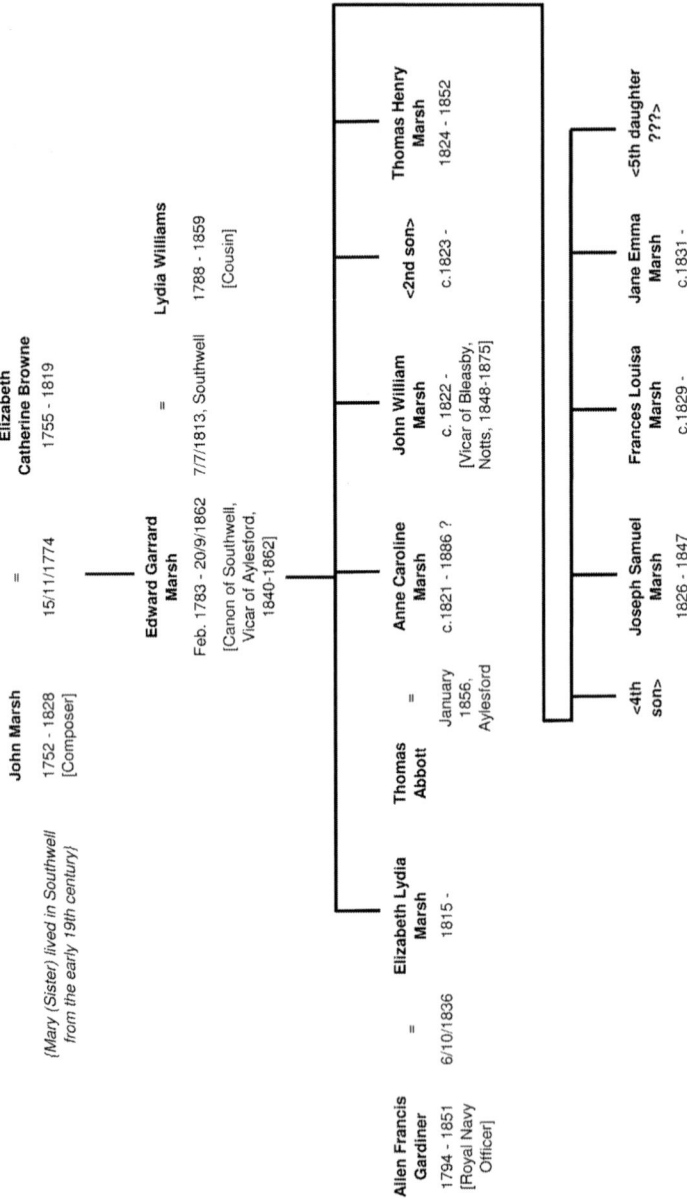

John Marsh
1752 - 1828
[Composer]

{Mary (Sister) lived in Southwell from the early 19th century}

= 15/11/1774

Elizabeth Catherine Browne
1755 - 1819

Edward Garrard Marsh
Feb. 1783 - 20/9/1862
[Canon of Southwell, Vicar of Aylesford, 1840-1862]

= 7/7/1813, Southwell

Lydia Williams
1788 - 1859
[Cousin]

Children:

Elizabeth Lydia Marsh
1815 -
= 6/10/1836
Allen Francis Gardiner
1794 - 1851
[Royal Navy Officer]

Anne Caroline Marsh
c.1821 - 1886 ?
= January 1856, Aylesford
Thomas Abbott

John William Marsh
c. 1822 -
[Vicar of Bleasby, Notts, 1848-1875]

<2nd son>
c.1823 -

Thomas Henry Marsh
1824 - 1852

Joseph Samuel Marsh
1826 - 1847

<4th son>

Frances Louisa Marsh
c.1829 -

Jane Emma Marsh
c.1831 -

<5th daughter>
???

Elizabeth Lydia Marsh compiled the "Records of the South American Missionary Society"
Anne Caroline Marsh (as Mrs Abbott) paid for the new organ in Aylesford Church in 1865

Appendix I

Relationships influencing music in Aylesford, 1860-1880

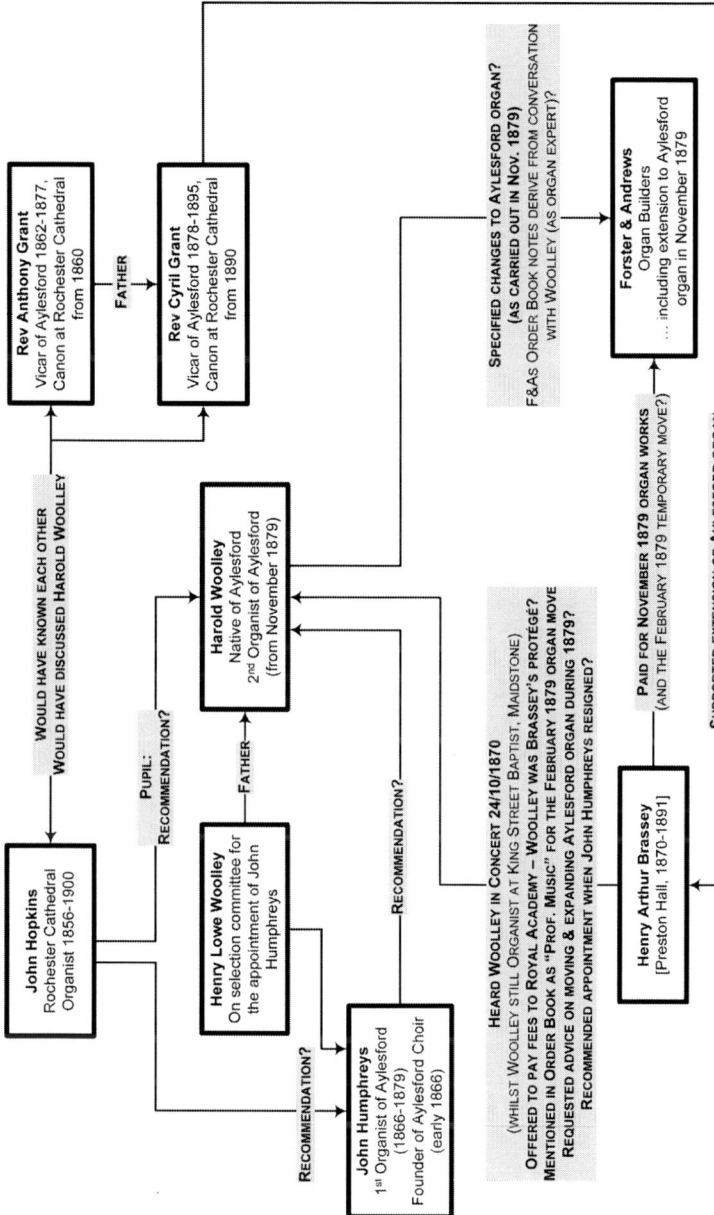

Rev Anthony Grant
Vicar of Aylesford 1862-1877, Canon at Rochester Cathedral from 1860

FATHER

Rev Cyril Grant
Vicar of Aylesford 1878-1895, Canon at Rochester Cathedral from 1890

SPECIFIED CHANGES TO AYLESFORD ORGAN? (AS CARRIED OUT IN NOV. 1879)
F&As ORDER BOOK NOTES DERIVE FROM CONVERSATION WITH WOOLLEY (AS ORGAN EXPERT)?

Forster & Andrews
Organ Builders
… including extension to Aylesford organ in November 1879

WOULD HAVE KNOWN EACH OTHER
WOULD HAVE DISCUSSED HAROLD WOOLLEY

John Hopkins
Rochester Cathedral Organist 1856-1900

PUPIL: RECOMMENDATION?

Harold Woolley
Native of Aylesford
2nd Organist of Aylesford (from November 1879)

Henry Lowe Woolley
On selection committee for the appointment of John Humphreys

FATHER

PAID FOR NOVEMBER 1879 ORGAN WORKS
(AND THE FEBRUARY 1879 TEMPORARY MOVE?)

SUPPORTED EXTENSION OF AYLESFORD ORGAN

Henry Arthur Brassey
[Preston Hall, 1870-1891]

RECOMMENDATION?

RECOMMENDATION?

HEARD WOOLLEY IN CONCERT 24/10/1870
(WHILST WOOLLEY STILL ORGANIST AT KING STREET BAPTIST, MAIDSTONE)
OFFERED TO PAY FEES TO ROYAL ACADEMY – WOOLLEY WAS BRASSEY'S PROTEGÉ?
MENTIONED IN ORDER BOOK AS "PROF. MUSIC" FOR THE FEBRUARY 1879 ORGAN MOVE
REQUESTED ADVICE ON MOVING & EXPANDING AYLESFORD ORGAN DURING 1879?
RECOMMENDED APPOINTMENT WHEN JOHN HUMPHREYS RESIGNED?

John Humphreys
1st Organist of Aylesford (1866-1879)
Founder of Aylesford Choir (early 1866)

Appendix J

Aylesford population, 1811–1901

Details from vestry minute book, 1736-1916 (held at Kent History and Library Centre, Maidstone).

Year	Inhabited Houses	Uninhabited Houses	Males	Females	Total Population
1811			341	534	875
1821	192	7	565	571	1136
1831	205		672	629	1301
1841	231	6	703	641	1344
1851			820	667	1487
1861	337	5	1154	898	2052
1871					2100
1881			1447	1267	2714
1891	560	15	1619	1318	2937
1901	553	15	1420	1258	2678

Families details as at July 1821

1821 age breakdown

Age group	Males	Females	Total
<5	81	94	175
5-10	88	63	151
10-15	70	75	145
15-20	58	65	123
20-30	70	89	159
30-40	55	65	120
40-50	44	40	84
50-60	48	45	93
60-70	30	16	46
70-80	13	16	29
80-90	8	3	11
Total	565	571	1136

Families trades as at July 1821

Employed in Agriculture	Employed in Trade	Other	Total
125	55	45	225

Appendix K

Current values of costs

Current values use the Money Sorter UK Inflation Calculator website (accessed 30/08/2015). Some rounding. Value since 2005 assumed unchanged.

www.moneysorter.co.uk/calculator_inflation2.html#calculator

Page	Date	Cost	Decimal	Value Now	Page	Date	Cost	Decimal	Value Now
18	1838	£158 11s 6d	£158.58	£12,500	70	1947	£120	£120.00	£3,300
20	1865	£12	£12.00	£1,000	70	1947	£20	£20.00	£550
21	1841	£2 2s	£2.10	£150	70	1947	£8	£8.00	£220
21	1841	£49 0s 11d	£49.05	£3,550	72	1837	£5	£5.00	£390
21	1862	£8 1s 8d	£8.08	£700	72	1846	£20	£20.00	£1,600
22	1862	£2 16s 8d	£2.83	£240	72	1848	£16	£16.00	£1,300
22	1862	£5 5s	£5.25	£450	72	1866	£10	£10.00	£800
22	1863	£160 1s 2d	£160.06	£14,000	72	1866	£30	£30.00	£2,500
22	1863	£130	£130.00	£11,500	73	1865	£25	£25.00	£2,200
22	1863	£2	£2.00	£175	73	1880	£57 4s	£57.20	£4,800
22	1863	£7 13s 3d	£7.66	£675	73	1882	£45	£45.00	£3,800
22	1863	£9 14s 2d	£9.71	£850	75	1890	£35	£35.00	£3,150
22	1863	8d	£0.03	£2.50	75	1894	£30	£30.00	£2,750
22	1863	£5 1s 4d	£5.07	£450	75	1894	£35	£35.00	£3,200
22	1863	£5 12s 5d	£5.62	£500	76	1896	£6 5s	£6.25	£600
23	1986	£6,935	£6,935.00	£14,200	76	1900	£7 10s	£7.50	£650
23	1988	£477.25	£477.25	£900	79	1907	£12 10s	£12.50	£1,050
23	1988	£160	£160.00	£300	79	1908	£7	£7.00	£600
23	1988	£36	£36.00	£65	79	1910	£20	£20.00	£1,650
24	1832	12s	£0.60	£48	79	1910	£25	£25.00	£2,060
24	1845	1s	£0.05	£4.25	80	1939	£30	£30.00	£2,500
31	1891	£1.045m	£1,045,000.00	£92,828,900	84	1864	£40	£40.00	£3,600
33	1878	£3,500	£3,500.00	£291,275	84	1864	£50	£50.00	£4,500
51	1865	£270	£270.00	£23,700	85	1893	£1 10s	£1.50	£135
51	1865	£13	£13.00	£1,140	85	1894	£2	£2.00	£182
53	1865	£270	£270.00	£23,700	85	1907	2s 6d	£0.13	£11
53	1865	£271 1s 0d	£271.05	£23,810	85	1950	£80	£80.00	£1,920
53	1865	£1 1s	£1.05	£90	85	1950	£100	£100.00	£2,400
53	1865	£20	£20.00	£1,750	85	1980	£800	£800.00	£2,400
54	1865	£250	£250.00	£21,950	85	1890	£3 1s 6d	£3.08	£280
54	1865	£20	£20.00	£1,750	85	1891	£4 4s 6d	£4.28	£380
54	1865	£270	£270.00	£23,700	85	1930	1d	£0.01	£0.25
54	1865	£13	£13.00	£1,138	85	1930	6d	£0.03	£1.40
56	1879	£95	£95.00	£8,250	85	1930	12s 6d	£0.53	£24
58	1879	£131	£131.00	£11,400	85	1939	£9 15s 6d	£9.78	£450
59	1879	£87	£87.00	£7,500	90	1961	£2	£2.00	£31
59	1879	£30	£30.00	£2,600	91	1955	£30	£30.00	£550
59	1879	£14	£14.00	£1,200	97	1963	£2,000	£2,000.00	£29,285
60	1890	£20	£20.00	£1,800	99	1964	£500	£500.00	£7,320
61	1894	£55 5s	£55.25	£5,000	99	1964	£4,000	£4,000.00	£56,675
61	1894	£19	£19.00	£1,700	100	1965	£340	£340.00	£4,600
61	1894	25s	£1.25	£110	102	1965	£3,933	£3,933.00	£53,250
61	1894	£30	£30.00	£2,725	102	1965	£1,800	£1,800.00	£24,370
62	1853	2£2s	£2.10	£187	103	1965	£200	£200.00	£2,710
62	1858	£2 2s	£2.10	£182	103	1966	£1,500	£1,500.00	£19,540
63	1895	£1 19s 6d	£1.98	£182	103	1966	£700	£700.00	£9,120
63	1895	£4	£4.00	£370	103	1966	£1,800	£1,800.00	£23,450
63	1894	£8 8s	£8.40	£765	103	1965	£2,120	£2,120.00	£28,700
63	1908	£30	£30.00	£2,500	107	1977	£16.32	£16.32	£71
66	1659	£300	£300.00	£50-£100K	108	1987	£4,585	£4,585.00	£9,020
67	1861	£6 15s	£6.75	£550	108	1987	£3,946.80	£3,946.80	£7,770
67	1861	1s 6d	£0.08	£6.66	108	1987	£2,000	£2,000.00	£3,930
67	1939	£3 19s	£3.95	£180	109	1987	£57.50	£57.50	£110
67	1946	£78 10s	£78.50	£2,300	109	1996	£1,850.63	£1,850.63	£2,425
68	1947	£150	£150.00	£4,100	111	1987	£741.75	£741.75	£1,460
69	1947	£90	£90.00	£2,450	111	1999	£519.94	£519.94	£630
69	1947	£150	£150.00	£4,100	112	2005	£23,000	£23,000.00	£24,000

Appendix L

Organ builders, maintainers etc

Builders

Date	Builder	Head Office	Summary
1838	Walker	London	Installation (2nd hand barrel organ)
1865	Forster & Andrews	Hull	Built (new organ)
1879	Forster & Andrews	Hull	Moved & extended
1894	Forster & Andrews	Hull	Extended
1908	Forster & Andrews	Hull	Cleaned
1947	Harvey	Maidstone	Modified
1965	NP Mander	London	Moved, rebuilt & extended
1987	NP Mander	London	Cleaned & overhauled
2015	FH Browne	Ash, nr. Canterbury	Rebuilt & extended

Notes:
Walker – Joseph Walker, likely Joseph William Walker (organ builders, established in 1828).
1838 (barrel) organ removed 1865, temporarily replaced by a harmonium (1863-65).
1840-62 – Also house organ (John Gray?) in Aylesford Vicarage.
1987 – Temporary provision of small pipe organ during rebuild.

Tuners / maintainers

From	To	Firm	Tuner
1853	1895	Thomas Goodwin (occasionally after 1865, possibly later than 1895?)	
1865	1909	Forster & Andrews	
1910	1964	Harvey	
1965	1977	NP Mander	R Beddoes
1977	1987	Wood Brown	Terry Wood
1987	2002	NP Mander	David Wintle
2002	2014	Mander Tunings	David Wintle
2015		FH Browne	

Organ blowers   *(Note: Very few records, thus list is incomplete)*

From	To	Name
1865	1870s?	?
c.1872	1880s?	? Mitchell (definitely 1/1/1872 - 11/2/1872)
1880s?	1900s	?
1909	1910s?	Alfred Wakefield
1910s?	mid 1930s	?
mid 1930s	early 1940s	Geoff Gay
early 1940s?	1947	Michael Gosling
1947		(Electric blower installed)

Appendix M

Acoustics: The impact of the organ in Aylesford Parish Church

Due to the acoustic properties of Aylesford church, and particularly the effect of the chancel arches in attenuating sound, a significant difference in the impact of the organ exists between the main body of the church and the chancel. In 1865, both organ and (integrated) console were positioned at the west end of the church; however, once the organ was moved to the North Aisle Chancel (Lady Chapel) in 1879, the perceived volume of the organ in the main body of the church would have been severely compromised; an attempt to address this was made with the addition of the Great Clarionet 8' in 1894. The effect was switched in 1965 when the organ returned to the main body of the church (the north aisle), but the console (now detached) remained in the Lady Chapel: The congregation benefitted from the organ at full power, whereas the organist's perception (and initially that of the choir too, until they moved) was one of a much quieter output than was the reality; further, there was a delay of approx. ¼ second between the organ and the console. The move of the console in 2015 to the north side of the choir stalls, in the nave, has finally addressed these issues.

A small set of acoustic tests were carried out by the author in 2010, and again after the rebuild in 2015, to demonstrate the impact of the building on the perception of the volume of the organ:

dBc Measurements	10/4/2010 (pre-rebuild, console in Lady Chapel)		13/8/2015 (post-rebuild and console move)	
Measurement Location	**Swell Flute 8', Pedal Bourdon 16'**	**Full Organ**	**Swell Flute 8', Pedal Bourdon 16'**	**Full Organ**
Console	71.2	95.8	74.2	97.2
Choir	79.5	94.5	79.5	95.0
Next to organ	80.5	97.5	80.5	97.7
Difference, console to choir	8.3	1.3	0.0	2.2

All measurements in dBc (as being considered the most appropriate measure of sound in a public venue).

Note on dBc *(courtesy of www.ehow.com):*
The C Filter: Measurements made using C filters are expressed in dBCs. Unlike dBA, its measurements suit low and high frequency sound levels. The C filter literally filters the sounds the microphone picks up in the sound level meter, used more in entertainment venues. The frequency response function, sometimes called a weighting characteristic, controls the tone by giving more weight to some frequencies than other less important frequencies. When transmitted sound has bass issues or problems, the C filter is typically used.

Appendix N

Recordings of the organ at Aylesford Parish Church

The earliest surviving recording of Aylesford Church organ dates back over 60 years, to 1953; most recent is a comprehensive recording of the organ, made immediately before the 2015 rebuild. Plans are in place to complete these set of recordings to demonstrate the organ after the 2015 rebuild. The following are the extant recordings of Aylesford organ:

- 1953: Harold Moore, playing Bach 'Jesu, joy of man's desiring' (BWV 147), and Walford Davies 'Solemn Melody' (recorded on 30/1/1953)
- c.1964: Harold Moore, playing Bach 'Fantasia in G' (BWV 572)
- c.1967: Harold Moore, organ recital
- 2011: Michael Keays, playing music used during a recital (including Thalben-Ball 'Elegy') (recorded 3/1/2011)
- 2014-2015: Michael Keays, playing a selection of music over four CDs (two recorded before the rebuild, two currently in production): Also included on around five hours of these total recordings are some of the historic recordings, and the 1965 talk by Noel Mander. The recordings will be available in 2016 from the author as a four CD set (proceeds will be used to support both the maintenance of the Aylesford organ and wider work of Aylesford church)

The organ was also sampled by Wyvern Organs, in April 2002.

A brief recording of the organ at St Mary's Church, Bleasby (ex-Aylesford Vicarage) was made by the author on 9/7/2002.

The opening talk for the 1965 rebuild of the Forster & Andrews organ, given by Noel Mander on 2/6/1965, was also recorded, and has been transcribed (although some recording quality issues have prevented a complete transcription).

Recordings of both the choir and organ are widespread, the following of which are the most significant:

- 29/9/1985: "Harvest Praise" service at Aylesford: First service of the author as organist at Aylesford, with a Welcome from the vicar (Rev Arthur Heathcote). Included as the voluntary Karg-Elert's "Nun Danket"
- May 1987: "Highway" (with Harry Secombe) (Television broadcast)
- Advent Sunday 1991: TVS morning service (1/12/1991) (Television broadcast)
- 1993: Whitsunday Evensong, Rochester Cathedral (30/5/1993) (Rochester Cathedral organ)
- November 1997: Commercial CD, with music by Michael J Keays (including the "Requiem")
- Many private recordings, including concerts (recorded by Ken Drury) and services, spanning the last 30 years, variously accompanied by Michael Keays and Helen Turner

Choir-only recordings include the following:

- May 1988: Telethon (television broadcast)
- 2000: Radio Kent carols (18/12/2000)

Appendix O

Fundraising for the 2015 organ restoration

In total, £54,135.00 was raised (including bank interest and reclaimed Gift Aid, where applicable) to fund the organ restoration, including console move, transportation and electrical costs. A wide variety of fundraising initiatives ran for a period of nearly seven years until the completion of the works in 2015.

It is with immense gratitude to the generosity of all those individuals and organisations who have contributed to the funding of this project, practically and financially, that the following lists capture the various fundraising initiatives:

Donations from corporates and organisations

A total of £16,354 was donated by the following:

Allchurches Trust
Aylesford Historical Society
Aylesford Parish Council
Aylesford Saturday Market (now Brassey Bazaar)
Aylesford School
Balancing Act Theatre
  (proceeds of "Murder, Mystery" play in church,
  September 2014)
Brassey Trust
Brook Concert Orchestra (Norman Blow)
Clarkes Funeral Services

East Surrey Organists Association
Family Funeral Service
Friends of Aylesford Church
Gallagher Group
Kent County Council
Kent County Organists Association
London Casinos International
Old Bridge Music Club
Rochester Bridge Trust
St Peter's School, Aylesford
Viner & Sons Ltd (Funeral Directors)

Fundraising Concerts

A total of £1,278.42 was raised through concerts by the following:

Aveley & Newham Brass Band Concert (25% of proceeds)
Brook Concert Orchestra (Concerts in church 6/10/2013 & 5/10/2014, & Christmas Carol services)
Community Concert
Innominata (11/5/2014)

Donations made 'in memoriam'

A total of £550 was donated in memory of the following (pipe designations shown in parenthesis):

Mrs Margaret J Dodd (Great Open Diapason 8' – C#, D, D#; Great Principal 4' – A;
  Great Twelfth 2⅔' – A)
Alan Gurr (Great Open Diapason 8' – A#)
Douglas Keays (Pedal Open Diapason 16' – DD)
Polly Narramore (Great Open Diapason 8' – AA#)
Jack Platt (Great Twelfth 2⅔' – CC)
Elsie Wells (Great Twelfth 2⅔' – AA)

Pipe sponsorship

"Preserve a Pipe" and "Adopt a Stop" donations amounted to £5,782.44. Donors are listed under the "Donations from individuals" (below), where anonymity has not been requested, or "Donations from Corporates and Organisations" (above); a log of the specific pipe and stop sponsorships is held with the 2015 organ restoration archive, and a copy placed inside the organ.

Sponsored events

Sponsored events, as listed below, raised a total of £7,955.68:

> Beetle drive
> Hymn singing (25/9/2011)
> Organathon (10/12/2011)
> > (Organists participating in the Organathon: Peter Bonnert; John Brown; Andrew Cesana; Malcolm Coates; Pauline Fisher; Beryl Fletcher; Roger Gentry; Peter Hart; Michael Keays; Brian Moore; Donald Preece; Karen Riches; Gary Tollerfield; Helen Turner; Keith Viner; Gavin Williams)
> Parachute jump, 6/10/2012 (Brenda Sladen)
> Sponsored 35-mile walk, 26/4/2014 (Michael Keays)
> Sponsored fast
> Sponsored voluntaries
> Talents scheme

Other fundraising activities

A total of £4,171.15 was raised from bank interest and through a number of initiatives and activities:

> Book donations
> Catering team
> Coins in a bottle
> Craft stall
> Crockery loan
> Eccles Ladies
> Flush fund balance
> > (residual amount remaining from the toilet / kitchenette fund)
>
> Flower arrangers
> Greetings cards
> Ladies lunch
> Line of pennies
> Plant sale
> Schools collections

… plus 25% of a series of general fundraising activities (e.g. Christmas Tree Festival, Quiz Night, Summer Fair)

Donations from individuals

Individual donations, including a coin collection, but excluding pipe or other sponsorships (noted above) raised an impressive £18,043.31:

> Martin Atkins
> John & Diane Atkinson
> Roy & Valerie Ballard
> Ann Beale
>
> Paul Bellamy
> Susie Birchall
> Richard & Cherith Bourne
> Alan & Sally Brailsford

Aaron Brann
Andrew & Ann Brown
Christopher Bubb
John Buckle
Lenny Bunn
Jean Caplin
Allan & Daphne Card
Malcolm & Brenda Clewer
Brian Coates
J Coates
Catherine Cogdell
Roy Cogger
Mr & Mrs S Collings
James & Lizzie Cook
Tim Cox
Betty Crouch
Carol Dawson
Katie Difford
Janet Dobson
Barbara Donohue
Bryan & Mary Dunmall
Brian Eddy
Brian Emery
John Etherton
Colin Evans
Valerie File
Geoff & Ann Game
Ann Gardner
Stuart & Lydia Gay
Mrs Grainer
Carol Grant
Marilyn Gurr
Bob & Joy Halliday
Peter Hanson
Dee Haynes
Janet Holdstock
Clare Hughes
Gordon & Barbara Hunt
Derrick & Margaret Jones
Michael & Anita Keays
Douglas Keays
Sandra Kings
Kevin Kings
E Knight

Paul Lee
Joe & Lin Lloyd
J Lunnon
Martin MacFarlane
Elizabeth Margerrison
Cyril Martin
Mike & Janet McConnell
Pauline McMunn
Dave Mockler
P A Moore
John Munro
Lawrence Munson
Heather Narramore
Phil & Annette Nobes
Michael Palin
John & Jenny Parker
B Parker
Charlotte Payne
P Platt
Aubrey Prentice
Jenny Relph
Angela Revis
E Richardson
Simon Robson
Betty Royall
Edward Sandford
R & R Sawyer
Peter & Penny Scrope
J Selby
Betty Sheldon
Chris Shuter
Norman Simister
Gordon & Brenda Sladen
John & Mary Smelt
John & Barbara Smith
Jonathan Smith
Peter Smith
Rita Smith
Wendy Smith
M Solway
Stella Stevenson
Jo Stirling
Pam Storr
Chris van Straaten

Michael Taylor	Robin & Helen Turner
Margaret Terry	Gerdine Vermeer
P Terry	Len & Elsie Wells
S Thompson	Miss M J Williams

… plus many more generous people who wish to remain anonymous.

Other fundraising approaches

The following lists other approaches which contributed to the fundraising already noted above:

"Be an Organ Donor" ("Put the heart back into our organ")
Calendars
"Cash in the Loft"
Church website progress updates
Direct mail
Display board
"Leave a Legacy"
Organ Appeal leaflet (professionally printed, and available as a PDF on the church website)
Press releases
Second hand toys and clothes sale
Talks and recitals by the organist

Appendix P

Sources and acknowledgements

Bibliography

CAST, Barbara: "The Church of Saint Mary's, Bleasby, Nottinghamshire – A brief guide" (1988 / 92)

ELVIN, Laurence: "Forster and Andrews Organ Builders, 1843-1956: A Chapter in English Organ Building" (1968)

FOSTER, Joseph: "Index Ecclesiasticus, 1800-1840" (1890)

HALE, Paul: "British Concert Organs" article in "Organists Review" (February 2002, p.25)

HALE, Paul: "The Organs and Organists of Rochester Cathedral" (c.1985)

HASTED, Edward: "The History and Topographical Survey of the County of Kent, Volume IV" (1798)

KEAYS, Michael: Detailed sketches and scale drawings, from observation and measurement in Aylesford Church, undertaken to support this edition.

MARSH, Rev J W (transcribed Beverley Wright): "A Farewell Address to the inhabitants of Bleasby, Morton and Halloughton" (22/9/1874)

McCRERIE, Alan: "Knowing Aylesford" (Copy, manually annotated "1974", but text suggests 1963-64)

ORDNANCE SURVEY Six Inch County Series 1895-1896 – Aylesford & Ditton

POWELL, Canon Henry: "Aylesford, where England began" (Manuscript, c.1960)

RAMSAY, Chris: "Nineteenth Century Urbanisation and the Anglican Church": www.anglicanism.org/admin/docs/nineteenthcenturyurbanisation.pdf

ROBINS, Brian: "The John Marsh Journals: The life and time of a gentleman composer (1752-1828)"

SEPHTON, James H: "Around Aylesford" (Tempus, 1999)

SEPHTON, James H: "Aylesford Society Journal, Vol. 1 No 3" (December 1994)

SEPHTON, James H: "Preston Hall, Aylesford" (1997)

SEPHTON, James H: "St Peter's Church of England Primary School" (Aylesford Society Manuscript, undated, c.1995)

SEPHTON, James H: "The Friars, Aylesford" (1999)

SEPHTON, James H: "The Parish Church, Aylesford" (Unpublished, draft)

SMETHAM, H: 'Rambles around Churches in the land of Dickens', Vol. IV. (Parrett & Neves, Chatham, 1929).

STURGEON, R: "Pictorial views of Aylesford, Eccles & Burham" (ENSO, 2010)

SUMNER, William L: "The Organ" (4th edition, Macdonald & Co, 1973)

THISTLEWAITE, Nicholas: "The Making of the Victorian Organ" (Cambridge University Press, 1990)

TURNER, Christopher: "When organists were dumb …" (article published in "Church Music Quarterly", RSCM, April 2000)

WALLS, Rev R W, AKC: "Short Description of the Church of Saint Peter in Aylesford" (undated, c.1945).

WELLS, Kenneth A E: Letters to Michael Keays (12/4/1987, 17/1/1988, 20/1/1988, 23/1/1988, 27/1/1988, 2/2/1988, 4/2/1988, 16/2/1988 & 23/4/1988)

WELLS, Kenneth A E: Letter to William (Linkstead?) (20/6/1986)

WELLS, Kenneth A E: "Preston Hall and its owners" (2nd edition, 1985, manuscript)

WILLIAMS, Rev Henry L: "Bleasby and its history" (1897)
(extracted from www.nottshistory.org.uk/monographs/bleasby1897/bleasby2.htm)

Documents

Archive records of NP Mander Ltd, and old tuning books, by kind permission of John Mander

Aylesford Church Choir Rules, c.1902, ref. P12/28/14, by kind permission of Kent History and Library Centre, Maidstone

Aylesford Church Minute Books 1916-1967 and 1967 onwards (Church office archive)

Aylesford Parish Magazines: Church office archive (by kind permission of Rev Arthur E Heathcote, William Linkstead and Anita Keays) and Kent History and Library Centre, Maidstone (by kind permission of Kent History and Library Centre, Maidstone)

British Newspaper Archive, copyright British Library Board (Bucks Herald, Dover Express, Maidstone Telegraph, Kent & Sussex Courier, Kentish Gazette, Sussex Agricultural Express)

History of Hampton Court (Vol II, 2nd edition, Bell, 1898) – Inventory of Oliver Cromwell (http://archive.org/stream/historyofhampton02laweuoft/historyofhampton02laweuoft_djvu.txt)

Log book and the "Bleasby Terrier" (Church inventory), St Mary's Church, Bleasby, by kind permission of Brian Temperley

Maidstone and Kentish Journal, and Maidstone Telegraph & West Kent Messenger (late 19th century): Kent History and Library Centre, Maidstone (by kind permission)

Report and Estimate on the Organ in the Parish Church of St Peter's Aylesford, Wm Hill & Son and Norman & Beard Ltd (30/9/1986) (written by Frank N Fowler)

The Times, News (p.3), 18/3/2006 (News International)

Old Vestry Books and Treasurers Records, by kind permission of Kent County Archives (now Kent History and Library Centre, Maidstone)

Individuals (conversations, technical information, recollections etc):

Stephen Bayley (FH Browne, organ builders)
Barbara Cast (Bleasby Church)
Laurence Elvin (Details from the records of Forster and Andrews)
Paul Hale (Rector Chori, Southwell Minster)
Rev Arthur E Heathcote
Paul Isom (Rochester DOA)
Bill Linkstead
Graham Lord (Wyvern Organs)
John Mander (NP Mander, organ builders)
Adam Rawlinson
John Smelt
Ray Sturgeon
Roy Taylor
Brian & Diana Temperley (Bleasby Church)
Gary Tollerfield
Jan Tollerfield
Tom W Tomkin
Michael Watcham (Photographs)
Len Wells
David Wintle (NP Mander Tunings)

Organisations

Aylesford Parish Council

Birmingham Central Library

British Institute of Organ Studies (BIOS)

British Organ Archive (BOA)

Hull History Centre: Facsimile copies of the ledger entries of Forster & Andrews (reproduced by kind permission)

Kent County Council, Business Intelligence Research & Evaluation: Business Intelligence Statistical Bulletin (Aylesford population figures)

Kent County Organists Association (KCOA)

Kent History and Library Centre, Maidstone: Text from the "Vestry Minute Book, Aylesford: 1736 – 1916 (19th August)" (reproduced by kind permission) [Records formerly held by Kent County Archives and Kent County Council Local Studies Library, Springfield, Maidstone, ref. P12/8/1]

Kent Messenger: Article on 1965 organ rebuild (reproduced by kind permission)

Royal School of Church Music (RSCM): Aylesford church choir affiliation dates

Websites

2011 Census (Aylesford population): www.kent.gov.uk/__data/assets/pdf_file/0016/8125/2011-Census-parish-population-bulletin.pdf

Acoustic measurement description: www.ehow.com

British History online (Nethersole House): www.british-history.ac.uk

Current money values: www.moneysorter.co.uk/calculator_inflation.html

Dates – Easter: www.dr-mikes-math-games-for-kids.com/easter-date-tables.html?century=19

Dates – Historic calendars: www.timeanddate.com/calendar

FH Browne, organ builders: www.fhbrowneandsons.co.uk

Kent Archaeology – Detailed description of monuments in Aylesford church: www.kentarchaeology.org.uk/Research

Kent Villages, Towns & Public Houses - History, Genealogy & Trade Directories – Traders in Melvilles 1858 Trade Directory: www.pubshistory.com/KentPubs

Maidstone Directory 1851: http://freepages.genealogy.rootsweb.ancestry.com/~mrawson/maiddir51.html

Marsh and Abbot family details: www.ancestry.co.uk

NP Mander, organ builders: www.mander-organs.com

National Archives (Hull History Centre listing of Forster & Andrews ledgers): www.nationalarchives.gov.uk

National Pipe Organ Register (NPOR): www.npor.org.uk

Personal dates validations: www.wikitree.com

UK Clergy List 1897: www.ancestry.co.uk

University of Leicester Special Collections Online: www.specialcollections.le.ac.uk (Kent Messenger Directory of Maidstone 1904 and Kelly's Directory of Kent, 1913. [Part 2: Private Resident & Trade Directories])

J W Walker, organ builders: www.jwwalker.co.uk/history.html

A note from the author

I express my grateful thanks to all the above individuals and organisations for their assistance and information, making specific mention of Jim Sephton, who was generous with his support and encouragement of this book; sadly, Jim passed away as the final drafts of this text were being written.

I also acknowledge and thank all individual and corporate fundraisers, who have provided both the ability to restore the organ at Aylesford, and the inspiration to record its rich history.

I would also thank and make specific mention of the following: Rev Christopher van Straaten, for his tireless enthusiasm and encouragement throughout the 2015 rebuild project, and for being a proof reader of this text; David Wintle of NP Mander Tuning Ltd, for his long-term care of the organ and technical information to assist this History; Steve Bayley and the team at FH Browne & Sons Ltd, who have proven that high quality craftsmanship still exists, and for patience with the author's enthusiasm and 'hands-on' approach during the 2015 rebuild. I am also grateful to Joseph Keays for the watercolour of the organ which graces the cover of this edition, and for my late father-in-law, Peter Goble, and Malcolm Martin, for the drawing of the organ which formed the cover of the first edition, and is reproduced in this edition. I am grateful for the Latin text which completes this book, translated "This organ was rebuilt to the greater glory of God, 2015"; this was supplied by an old school friend, Simon May (Head of Classics at St Paul's School, London).

Helen Turner has supported not just the 2015 rebuild project, but the music at Aylesford Church itself for nearly half a century: With playing, singing and leading (particularly of the Junior Choir), Aylesford Church is heavily indebted to her skill and dedication, and my job as organist and choirmaster would have been considerably more difficult without Helen's support. Robin Turner too has been a key driver in the 2015 restoration, alongside Alan Longmuir, and both have helped encourage the support of Aylesford Church PCC and congregation, without which the 2015 rebuild would never have occurred. Fundraising organisation and efficiency was greatly assisted by Claire Sullivan, Gordon Hunt, Gerry Hughes and Pam Storr; I record my thanks to them for their important role in the latest restoration project.

John Devlin, at The Design Practice in Maidstone, has provided the brilliant design ideas which have lifted the whole of this work to a new level, and made it considerably more readable! I would also like to thank Oliver Kleinman from Orbital Print for the production of a fine quality book.

And finally … there is one person who has patiently put up with all the paperwork accumulating around the house for the last 30 years, assisted with research (especially in making documents available in the church office), proof-read both editions (and making useful suggestions), and generally adapted to living with an organ 'anorak', particularly for the last ten years whilst the 2015 rebuild project has been running. I am greatly indebted to Anita, my wife, for supporting me in my role of organist at Aylesford Church and in the running of the 2015 rebuild project, and also in enabling me to compile this updated History of the Organ at St Peter & St Paul's Church, Aylesford, which I dedicate to the Parishioners of Aylesford Church and the Organ Appeal Fundraisers, as a comprehensive record of the past to inspire and inform future generations.

Michael J Keays

Michael was born in Kingswinford, Staffordshire, in 1959, moving to Tettenhall, Wolverhampton, at the age of three. Educated at Wolverhampton Grammar School, and a member of the Choir of St Peter's Collegiate Church, Wolverhampton (under the inspirational direction of Brian Armfield), Michael was taught the organ by David Rendell, now Organist Emeritus at St Peter's. At the age of 20, Michael moved to London, to undertake a Theology degree at Kings College, London, becoming Organ Scholar there in 1982. Michael graduated, with a BD AKC, in 1983.

Whilst at Kings, Michael met Anita: Married in 1982, Michael and Anita now have three grown-up children and one grand-child. After some time at St John's, Edmonton, Michael was appointed organist and choirmaster at St Peter & St Paul's Church Aylesford, Kent, in September 1985, where he is assisted by Helen Turner. Michael has managed a number of IT projects for the BBC, BBC World Service and ITV, with extensive experience in both the telecoms and broadcast sectors, and since 2015 has been a director of FH Browne & Sons (organ builders). With music being the primary external activity, Michael also has a keen interest in local history, pipe organs, steam trains, cricket and motor sport.

HOC ORGANUM
ANNO DOMINI MMXV
EST REFECTUM AD
MAIOREM DEI GLORIAM